Essentials

W9-AYJ-830

of PSYCHOLOGICAL ASSESSMENT *Series*

Everything you need to know to administer, interpret, and score the major psychological tests.

I'd like to order the following
ESSENTIALS OF PSYCHOLOGICAL ASSESSMENT:

- ❏ WAIS-III Assessment / 28295-2 / $34.95
- ❏ CAS Assessment / 29015-7 / $34.95
- ❏ Millon Inventories Assessment / 29798-4 / $34.95
- ❏ Forensic Psychological Assessment / 33186-4 / $34.95
- ❏ Bayley Scales of Infant Development-II Assessment / 32651-8 / $34.95
- ❏ Myers-Briggs Type Indicator® Assessment / 33239-9 / $34.95
- ❏ WISC-III and WPPSI-R Assessment / 34501-6 / $34.95
- ❏ Career Interest Assessment / 35365-5 / $34.95
- ❏ Rorschach Assessment / 33146-5 / $34.95
- ❏ Cognitive Assessment with KAIT and Other Kaufman Measures 38317-1 / $34.95
- ❏ MMPI-2 Assessment / 34533-4 / $34.95
- ❏ Nonverbal Assessment / 38318-X / $34.95
- ❏ Cross-Battery Assessment / 38264-7 / $34.95

Please send this order form with your payment (credit card or check) to:
JOHN WILEY & SONS, INC., Attn: J. Knott, 10th Floor
605 Third Avenue, New York, N.Y. 10158-0012

Name _____

Affiliation _____

Address _____

City/State/Zip _____

Phone   E-mail

- ❏ Would you like to be added to our e-mailing list?

Credit Card: ❏ MasterCard   ❏ Visa   ❏ American Express
(All orders subject to credit approval)

Card Number _____

Exp. Date   Signature

TO ORDER BY PHONE, CALL 1-800-225-5945
Refer to promo code #1-4081
To order online: www.wiley.com/essentials

Essentials

of Rorschach Assessment

Tara Rose

Nancy Kaser-Boyd

Michael P. Maloney

 John Wiley & Sons, Inc.

NEW YORK • CHICHESTER • WEINHEIM • BRISBANE • SINGAPORE • TORONTO

Copyright © 2001 by John Wiley & Sons, Inc. All rights reserved.
Published simultaneously in Canada.

Library of Congress Cataloging-in-Publication Data:
Rose, Tara.
    Essentials of Rorschach assessment / Tara Rose, Nancy Kaser-Boyd, Mike Maloney.
        p.   cm. — (Essentials of psychological assessment series)
    Includes bibliographical references (p.   ) and index.
    ISBN 0-471-33146-5 (pbk. alk. paper)
    1. Rorschach Test   I. Kaser-Boyd, Nancy   II. Maloney, Michael.
III. Title.   IV. Series.
  BF698.8.R5R67   2000
    155.2'842—dc21   00-038209
                                                                                    CIP

Printed in the United States of America.
10   9   8   7   6   5   4   3   2   1

CONTENTS

I n the *Essentials of Psychological Assessment* series, we have attempted to provide the reader with books that will deliver key practical information in
the most efficient and accessible style. The series features instruments in
a variety of domains, such as cognition, personality, education, and neuro-
psychology. For the experienced clinician, books in the series will offer a
concise, yet thorough, way to master utilization of the continuously evolving
supply of new and revised instruments, as well as a convenient method for
keeping up to date on the tried-and-true measures. The novice will find here
a prioritized assembly of all the information and techniques that must be at
one's fingertips to begin the complicated process of individual psychological
diagnosis.

Wherever feasible, visual shortcuts to highlight key points are utilized
alongside systematic, step-by-step guidelines. Chapters are focused and suc-
cinct. Topics are targeted for an easy understanding of the essentials of administration, scoring, interpretation, and clinical application. Theory and research are continually woven into the fabric of each book, but always to
enhance clinical inference, never to sidetrack or overwhelm. We have long
been advocates of "intelligent" testing—the notion that a profile of test
scores is meaningless unless it is brought to life by the clinical observations
and astute detective work of knowledgeable examiners. Test profiles must be
used to make a difference in the child's or adult's life, or why bother to test?
We want this series to help our readers become the best intelligent testers
they can be.

In *Essentials of Rorschach Assessment*, Tara Rose and Drs. Kaser-Boyd and Maloney organize Exner Comprehensive System material from a number of
sources—the Rorschach Workbook, Exner's *Comprehensive System* volumes,
and other interpretive texts—into an easy to use handbook. Written for the

Rorschach beginner, this book presents scoring and interpretation guidelines in a simple, easy to read format, and shows how the Rorschach can be applied to common referral questions. Annotated references are provided to guide independent study on advanced interpretation and psychometric issues.

Alan S. Kaufman, Ph.D., and Nadeen L. Kaufman, Ed.D., Series Editors
Yale University School of Medicine

One

OVERVIEW

Adrienne C. Davis, Ph.D.

The assessment of "personality," where personality is broadly defined as the characteristic way in which a person perceives the world, relates to others, solves problems, regulates emotions, manages stress, and copes with life's challenges, is an integral part of the process by which mental health professionals evaluate, understand, and ultimately treat their patients. The assumption is that there are enduring patterns of thinking, feeling, and behaving—some adaptive, some maladaptive—that are characteristic of each of us, and that these patterns can be identified with the use of psychological tests. The Rorschach Inkblot Test is one of a wide array of personality assessment procedures available for this purpose. Personality tests vary with respect to structure and content. At one end of the spectrum are highly structured tests with carefully selected questions and a limited range of possible responses that are objectively administered and scored. At the other end of the spectrum are tests that are referred to as *projective* personality tests. This latter group of tests, of which the Rorschach is one, is less structured, allows for a variety of responses, and exposes the subject to ambiguous stimuli. These projective tests are believed to access the deeper layers of personality structure and perhaps the complexities of personality dynamics. Some personality tests are broad based in that they attempt to provide a comprehensive view of the subject's personality dynamics. Results from these tests purport to provide a psychological picture of the "whole person." The Rorschach is such a test. Other personality tests are less ambitious and focus on particular aspects of the personality, perhaps those aspects that can be more directly observed or measured, like the subject's mood, level of anxiety, problem-solving techniques, frustration tolerance, or responses to stress. Suffice it to say, there are measures of personality that can be found for nearly every purpose. However, they vary widely with respect to format, scoring, validity, reliability, standardization, and popularity. One of the goals of this book is to provide a clear and concise yet comprehensive reference for those who want to understand and use the Rorschach Inkblot Test with confidence. Particular emphasis is placed on the assessment of adult personality via Exner's Comprehensive System (Exner, 1993).

Essentials of Rorschach Assessment is one in a series of books that provide the basic elements of various assessment instruments for the beginner in an easy-to-read format. This book is structured so that issues related to administration, scoring, interpretation, and application of the Rorschach are emphasized using Exner's scoring system. Each chapter is written with the first-time administrator in mind and, as such, provides easy-to-follow, step-by-step instructions. In addition, the instructions are referenced to the corresponding page numbers in volume 1 of Exner's *Comprehensive System* (1993). This volume is not meant to replace the very extensive coverage of the Rorschach technique summarized in Exner's three volumes; it is meant to simplify and clarify many details of the test. Moreover, those who read this book and would like a more in-depth review are referred to the reference section at the end of the book. Chapters include "Rapid Reference," "Caution," and "Don't Forget" boxes, which highlight the important points and can be referred back to easily. At the end of each chapter, questions are provided as a summary and review of the information that has been covered.

HISTORY OF THE RORSCHACH TECHNIQUE

If there is one word that describes the Rorschach, it is *controversial*. Even during the early 1900s when Hermann Rorschach first began developing the idea of characterizing the unique responses of different types of clinical populations, his efforts received mixed and sometimes highly critical reviews from his colleagues in Europe. What makes the history of this test all the more intriguing is the fact that much of the research and development of the Rorschach has occurred during the decades following Rorschach's premature death in 1922 at the age of 37. However, despite a long history of controversy and lingering debate regarding the reliability and application of the Rorschach procedure, to the dismay of its critics and the applause of its devotees, the Rorschach has developed into one of the most popular methods for assessing adult personality. A survey conducted by Watkins, Campbell, Nieberding, and Hall-mark (1995) of over 400 clinicians revealed that 82% used the Rorschach regularly in their practice. Moreover, the Rorschach ranked 4th among assessment procedures employed. Only the WAIS/WAIS-R/WAIS-III, MMPI/MMPI-2, and Sentence Completion tests were used more often.

Hermann Rorschach was a Swiss-born physician whose first and only manuscript about this test, *Psychodiagnostik,* published in June 1921, described the Rorschach procedure that he developed between 1909 and 1913 as a psychiatric resident at Munsterlingen Mental Hospital in Russia. His procedure for exploring perceptual and psychological processes was influenced by, among other things, the Word Association Test that was developed by psychoanalyst Carl Jung. In his early studies Rorschach compared the responses of psychotic patients on Jung's Association Test with those on the inkblot "test" and concluded that the two tests were tapping somewhat different psychological processes. Rorschach did not conceive of his technique as a "test" per se but as an empirically based tool for differentiating the responses of varied groups, including mentally retarded, schizophrenics, and other groups with known characteristics. He believed that perceptual processes—how people organize and structure what they see—are closely linked to aspects of the human psyche. Since the major symptoms demonstrated by schizophrenics, the clinical population with which he worked, involve disorders of thought and perception, it follows that Rorschach would explore procedures to gain better insight into this disorder.

According to Ellenberger (1954), Rorschach saw himself first and foremost as a scientist and was most interested in pursuing a career in clinical research, not clinical practice. His development of the inkblot technique was empirically based. So, it is of interest to note, that some of the strongest critics of the Rorschach are those in academia and proponents of empirically based diagnostic and treatment techniques who view the Rorschach technique as not empirically based.

Rorschach was not the first or only person to explore the diagnostic use of inkblots (see Rapid Reference 1.1). According to Klopfer and Davidson (1962), the first recorded discussion of inkblots was in a paper published by Justinus Kerner in Germany in 1857, who noted in his article the many objects that can be observed in inkblots. Later, in 1895, Alfred Binet, who developed one of the first intelligence tests, noted that inkblots could be used

≡ *Rapid Reference 1.1*

Early History of the Inkblot Technique

Year	Investigator	Research Contribution
1857	Kerner	Visual imagination
1895	Binet	Imagination
1897	Dearborn	Imagination
1900	Kirkpatrick	Speed of associations
1910	Whipple	First standardized set of inkblots
1917	Parsons	Imagination
	Hens	Imagination among children
1921	Rorschach	Perception and personality
		Differential diagnosis of schizophrenia

to examine imagination in children. After the turn of the century, in both the United States and Europe, several other inkblot investigators would follow, including Dearborn (1897), Kirkpatrick (1900), Whipple (1910), and Parsons (1917). The focus of their research was the imaginative process. It is unknown to what extent Rorschach knew of or was influenced by these investigators; however, Rorschach is also said to have used inkblots to determine whether gifted students showed more fantasy or imagination than less gifted students. Moreover, interest in inkblots seemed to blossom during a period of history when the game of Klecksography was popular among children. Klecksography involved making inkblots on a piece of paper, and then folding and arranging the inkblot in order to give it a particular form. Participants would compete by trying to generate the most elaborate responses. It is assumed that Rorschach himself played this game as a child. Reportedly, he was given the nickname Klec ("inkblot") by his friends, presumably because of his early fascination with inkblots (Ellenberger, 1954).

In 1917 the Polish psychiatrist Szymon Hens developed and published an inkblot test as his doctoral dissertation. Rorschach's knowledge of Hens's inkblot test is believed to have spurred his commitment to his own inkblot technique after he had set aside the project for several years to pursue other professional goals (Ellenberger, 1954). The early publications of the inkblot technique, those pre-dating the work of Rorschach, focused on the content of inkblot responses, and little consideration was given to the possible relationship between responses to inkblots and personality dynamics. It is clear that unique among Rorschach's contributions was his focus on the structure of the responses given, in other words, *how* responses were seen and their relationship to personality. In their book on content interpretation, Aronow and Reznikoff (1976) note that the last question Rorschach wished to answer was "What does the subject see?" Of much greater import to Rorschach was which factors or features of the inkblot determined the subject's response.

The basic assumption underlying the Rorschach is that there is a relationship between *perception* and *personality* (Klopfer & Davidson, 1962). The classification of the Rorschach as a "projective" test did not originate with Hermann Rorschach. It was Frank (1939) who proposed the "projective hypothesis" and included the Rorschach in his review of projective personality tests. Since ambiguous stimuli like inkblots allow for multiple responses and are believed to elicit unconscious *projections* of the subject's own unconscious needs, conflicts, motivations, and the like, the Rorschach is generally considered a projective test. Moreover, the interpretation of Rorschach responses is based on the premise that the manner in which the subject organizes his or her responses to the inkblots is representative of how they organize and respond to the world in general.

It was Rorschach's contention that fundamental aspects of the subject's psychological functioning with respect to cognitive/intellectual abilities, affective or emotional style, feelings about self and others, and ego functioning (including areas of psychological conflict and defenses) are revealed in the process by which the subject organizes the inkblot into a response. As noted earlier, Rorschach was most interested in uncovering what features of the inkblot determined the subject's response. The response itself was of much less importance to Rorschach. Therefore, the scoring and interpretation of a Rorschach protocol or set of responses to the inkblots focuses on the manner in which the subject arrived at a particular response, that is, by way of its form, color, shading, movement, texture, and so on. Rapid Reference 1.2 provides a summary of fundamental Rorschach concepts.

≡ *Rapid Reference 1.2*

The Rorschach: Fundamental Concepts

- Derived from the "inkblot" technique of studying imagination and creativity
- Developed by a physician, Hermann Rorschach, to understand the relationship between perception and personality
- A projective personality test designed to reveal underlying personality structure
- Five scoring systems have been developed; Exner's Comprehensive System is most often taught and psychometrically sound.
- Interpretation is based on *how* the subject arrives at his or her response; content is secondary.

THE DEVELOPMENT OF THE RORSCHACH TECHNIQUE

During the years following Rorschach's death in 1922, several scoring systems were developed. These scoring systems have generated the greatest amount of controversy about the Rorschach—that is, the variability of the scoring and the nature of the interpretations that can be reliably made. There was also concern about the extent to which these scoring and interpreting systems remained true to Rorschach's original concept of the nature and value of the inkblot procedure. However, by 1957, five unique scoring systems had evolved, the most popular of which were developed by Beck (1937) and Klopfer (1937). The fundamental assumptions of these systems were in conflict with each other. Beck attempted to adhere closely to Rorschach's method of coding and scoring and his belief that responses to the inkblots involved a cognitive-perceptual process. Beck also stressed the importance of establishing strong empirical relationships between Rorschach scoring codes and outside criterion measures, again, consistent with Rorschach's original thinking and purpose. Klopfer, on the other hand, was closely aligned with the psychoanalytic principles of Freud and Jung and therefore he emphasized the symbolic nature of a subject's responses because, theoretically, it reflects the reservoir of the subject's unconscious needs, motives, feelings, and conflicts. Klopfer focused his scoring and interpretation on response *content*. As such, Klopfer's system was considered a major deviation from Rorschach's original intention for this procedure. Response content was an area in which Rorschach was least interested. Three other coding systems, developed by Piotrowski (1957), Hertz (1934), and Rapaport, Gill, and Schafer (1946), were also in use and represented a middle ground between Beck and Klopfer (Groth-Marnat, 1997). The existence of different theoretical approaches to the Rorschach and scoring systems led to much confusion and ambiguity with respect to its interpretation and therefore its usefulness. During the decades that followed, the Rorschach received much criticism in the psychological and psychiatric communities, both constructive and hostile. At one point, it was recommended that students not waste their time studying it. Among the challenges to the Rorschach technique have been its poor psychometric properties, the questionable empirical basis of the interpretations, the methodological flaws involved in research on the Rorschach, and the lack of standardized procedures for administration and scoring. In addition, there have been challenges to the very theoretical foundation on which the Rorschach is based. Moreover, early studies did not adequately consider the influence of intelligence, socioeconomic status, age, and education on a subject's response productivity and perhaps the kind of responses given (Exner, 1969, 1983).

RECENT DEVELOPMENTS

During the late 1960s and early 1970s, it was John Exner who formally addressed many criticisms of the Rorschach at the Rorschach Research Foundation (later called the Rorschach Workshops), which he started in 1968. One of the major goals of the foundation was to determine which of the five existing scoring systems demonstrated the greatest empirical sturdiness and clinical utility. After a meta-analysis of the various ex-

---

DON'T FORGET 1.1

Improvements in the Rorschach Technique

- Creation of a foundation to formally study the Rorschach technique
- Larger normative database
- Standardized administration procedures
- Development of a consistent scoring system
- Special scoring categories
- Empirically based interpretations
- Inclusion of research control groups for age, gender, IQ, and socioeconomic status

isting systems, Exner concluded that the research and clinical use of the Rorschach was seriously flawed and he endeavored to improve both and thereby regain respectability for the Rorschach procedure (see Don't Forget 1.1). Exner and his colleagues began by collecting a large, broad, normative database. In addition, they established clear guidelines for seating, verbal instructions, recording of responses, and inquiring about the examinee's responses. With respect to scoring and interpretation, Exner did not create an entirely new scoring system; rather he incorporated the most sound elements of the existing scoring systems into one comprehensive system. In addition, he added several special scoring categories that provided a more complete assessment of the personality in terms of both trait and state aspects—that is, those aspects of personality that are more engrained and endure across time and situations, and those that are more transient and influenced by situations factors. Exner's *Rorschach: A Comprehensive System* was published in 1974. An expanded edition of this volume was published in 1983 and a third edition was published in 1993. Two additional volumes have been published. Volume 2, published in 1978 and updated in 1991, focused on Rorschach interpretation, and volume 3, published in 1982 and updated in 1995, focused on the use of the Rorschach with children and adolescents.

Despite the criticisms and potential limitations inherent in the Rorschach as a projective test, it continues to be a popular test instrument for a variety of reasons. It is easy to handle and administer, it generates a huge amount of data about the subject, and it is believed to have the ability to bypass the subject's conscious resistances and thereby assess underlying personality structure, particularly subjects with borderline psychopathology. The Rorschach is thought to be highly resistant to faking—that is, the subject purposely exaggerating or otherwise distorting his or her responses. Moreover, with the continuing contributions of Exner and his colleagues to improve the psychometric properties of the Rorschach, it is considered a valuable assessment instrument when used by a trained examiner. As noted earlier, despite its modest beginnings as a descriptive research tool, the Rorschach has evolved into an instrument that provides a comprehensive assessment of basic aspects of psychological functioning. Finally, the Rorschach Inkblot Test is one of the most researched assessment instruments available and, as such, the quality, strength, and integrity continue to evolve and improve.

RORSCHACH DESCRIPTION AND PROCEDURE

The standard set of 10 inkblots, originally selected by Rorschach, are still in use today. Each inkblot is nearly symmetrical and centered on a piece of $6\frac{3}{4}"$ × $9\frac{1}{2}"$ cardboard. There are five achromatic or black-and-white cards (I, IV, V, VI, and VII) and five chromatic or colored cards (II, III, VIII, IX, and X). Cards II and III are black and red only. Each inkblot has unique characteristics in terms of design, color, shading, and texture, and tends to provoke typical responses.

The Rorschach is individually administered in two phases, a response phase and an inquiry phase. The first phase involves a verbatim recording of each response to the ten inkblots. The second phase, which involves asking the examinee to explain how he or she saw each response, is used to clarify the examinee's responses so that each response can be scored or coded accurately. Throughout this process, only structured questions to clarify how the subject formed his or her perception are allowed.

The Rorschach consists of several scoring categories: *location* (where on the inkblot the response was seen), *determinants* (what features of the inkblot determined what was seen), *form level* (how well the response fits the blot area), *content* (what was seen); and the *popularity* or *originality* of the response (see Rapid Reference 1.3). The coding of determinants is often considered the most challenging and the most

Rapid Reference 1.3

Major Rorschach Scoring Categories

- Location: what area of the inkblot was used to form the response?
- Determinants: what features of the inkblot determined what was seen?
- Form level: how well does the response fit the blot area?
- Content: what was seen?
- Popularity-originality: how common is the response/concept seen by other subjects?
- Organizational activity: describe the efficiency with which the subject organizes a stimulus field.

subject to error because this category has the most possibilities: form, movement, color, space, shading, texture, dimension, pairs, and reflection. In addition to the core scoring categories, Exner developed 14 special scoring categories that identify atypical and possibly thought-disordered aspects of the subject's responses. These categories include codes for unusual verbalizations, perseveration and integration failure, special content characteristics, personalized answers, and special color phenomena.

After the responses given for each card are recorded verbatim, the sequence of responses is tabulated and the responses are scored or coded. These scores are summarized in the Structural Summary, a form that is composed of two sections. In the first section of the summary the frequencies of scores or codes are recorded—the total number of whole (W) responses, the total number of movement (M) responses, the total number of pure color (C) responses, the total number of special scores, and so on. The second section of the summary form includes various ratios, percentages, and derivations that are calculated from the frequencies obtained in the first part of the summary. These ratios reflect various psychological factors such as ideation, modulation of affect, interpersonal relatedness, and self-perception, as well as special indices such as schizophrenia and suicide potential. Rorschach interpretations regarding personality functioning arise from these calculations.

The interpretation of the Rorschach is a two-stage process. The first stage, the propositional stage, involves generating a hypothesis about the subject based on a careful review of the main components of the structural summary. The second stage, the integration stage, involves developing a description of the subject based on the modification or clarification of the hypothesis that was generated. Don't Forget 1.2 summarizes the description and administration of the Rorschach.

THEORETICAL AND RESEARCH FOUNDATION

As noted earlier, the Rorschach is considered a projective personality assessment technique. Projective techniques are described as such because they are believed to assess our unconscious perceptions, thought processes, needs, motivations, and conflicts. It seems to follow that a technique like the Rorschach relies on certain psychoanalytic principles, for example, the unconscious and the defense mechanism of projection. Because a relatively unstructured test like the Rorschach has no right or wrong answers, the respondent must utilize his or her own unique inner experiences and perceptions to organize the inkblot into something meaningful and generate a response. However, Exner argues that the Rorschach is not primarily a projective test and that most responses do not show evidence of projection. For example, some of the inkblots have a more definite form and are easier to respond to; responses such as "bat" or "butterfly" to Card V are easy to generate and therefore do not reflect the process of projection. According to Exner, projections and psychopathology are manifested in the embellishments to the responses. So, the response "a bat, like when I visited a cave in Arizona and they were flying around, that was scary" may reflect projection on the part of the subject.

> # DON'T FORGET 1.2
>
> ## Rorschach Description and Administration
>
> - The Rorschach is administered individually.
> - A standard set of 10 inkblots is used, each with unique characteristics.
> - There are two phases to the administration: the Association Phase and the Inquiry Phase.
> - An extensive scoring system incorporates elements from older systems with newer elements of Exner and his colleagues.
> - Responses are tabulated, scored, and summarized on the Structural Summary Form.
> - There is a two-stage interpretation process: the Propositional Stage and the Integration Stage.
> - Use of the Rorschach requires extensive training and practice.

Rorschach initially developed this instrument as a tool for describing the functioning of persons with different types of mental disorders, with the assumption that patients with certain types of mental disorders will organize their responses in a distinct and identifiable manner. However, the use of the Rorschach has progressed well beyond this modest beginning. As Weiner (1997) points out, "The Rorschach is a multifaceted method of generating structural, thematic and behavioral data" (p. 6). In this regard, the process by which a response is selected and delivered is significant in its own right. According to Exner, when an individual first looks at an inkblot many potential responses come to mind, very few of which are ultimately offered. The subject then decides which responses to offer and discards the rest. Responses are selected or discarded based on *economy* (there are too many potential responses to deliver them all); *censorship* (the response is perceived as not appropriate to say); the subject's *personality traits or styles;* or due to the *psychological state* of the subject caused by the demands of the task, for example, anxiety, depression, or stress. A fundamental assumption of the Rorschach technique is that basic psychological characteristics of the examinee play a dominant role in determining which of the potential answers will be delivered (Exner, 1983).

STANDARDIZATION AND PSYCHOMETRIC PROPERTIES

With Exner's development of the Comprehensive System came a greatly expanded normative database for which he provided extensive descriptive statistics (Exner, 1993). Briefly, his database includes 700 adult nonpatients stratified to represent the 1980 census, and 1,390 children and adolescents. His patient reference groups included 320 schizophrenics, 315 hospitalized depressives, 440 outpatients with various diagnoses, and 180 patients with character disorders.

As noted earlier, with the early development of several different scoring methods, the reliability of Rorschach interpretations fell under criticism. The Comprehensive System has since not only standardized the administration procedures but also brought consistency to the coding and scoring and, therefore, the interpretation of Rorschach responses. Much of the research on the psychometric properties of the Rorschach focuses on inter-rater reliability in scoring, or, the extent to which the scoring by two independent raters of the same protocol is consistent. This is an important area of focus since accurately and consistently scored protocols improve the consistency with which interpretations can be made across clinicians.

In his review of the major scoring systems, Exner (1969) only included a scoring code if it had at least .85 inter-rater reliability. Subsequent research (Weiner, 1997) has found inter-rater reliability greater than 90% for location scores, pairs, popular responses, and Z scores (a score that reflects organizational activity). For determinants and special scores, reliability coefficients are in the mid-80s. Exner has also provided test-retest reliability data (whereby subjects are administered the test at two different points in time), ranging from 7 days to 3 years. After the longest period of time (3 years), 13 of the core variables showed stability coefficients greater than or equal to .80. The categories with the lowest stability coefficients tended to be those measuring psychological states such as anxiety that can fluctuate over time. Exner has also found fluctuations in the Rorschach protocols of children, and he presents data that shows the effect of cognitive development on several important Rorschach scores. Exner's findings help to support the contention among developmental theorists that the cognitive processes of children change as children mature.

The reliability of scoring and test-retest reliability has received more attention than test validity. However, Weiner (1996) summarized some of the most relevant studies regarding the Rorschach's validity. Weiner's review of two meta-analytic studies by Parker, Hanson, and Hunsley (1988) and Atkinson (1986) suggest that the Rorschach technique is conceptually valid when "used in the manner for which it was designed and intended" (Weiner, 1996, p. 208). In this same study by Parker and his colleagues, validity data was found to be comparable to that of the Minnesota Multiphasic Personality Inventory (MMPI). The results of these studies have to do with the *overall validity* of the instrument not the validity of specific scores and categories. Weiner (1996) also provides data indicating that the Rorschach Inkblot Method, as he refers to it, has shown success in differentiating trait and state personality variables, measuring developmental change in children and adolescents, monitoring improvement in psychotherapy, and identifying experienced distress in war veterans with PTSD. To review specific studies consult the reference section of this volume. In addition, Rapid Reference 1.4 provides an overview of the Rorschach Inkblot Test, including testing information, examiner qualifications, and publication information.

COMPREHENSIVE REFERENCES

The Life and Work of Hermann Rorschach (Ellenberger, 1954) provides a detailed and intimate account of the life of the test's developer. The three volumes of Exner's *Rorschach: A Comprehensive System* (1991, 1993, 1995) provide in-depth information about the strengths and weaknesses of the Rorschach technique, including its psychometric properties, scoring, interpretation, and recent research developments as well as a review of the major scoring systems. Volume 1, in its third edition, provides the background of the original formulation of the comprehensive system and is the primary source for all aspects of

≡ Rapid Reference 1.4

Rorschach Inkblot Test

Author: Hermann Rorschach, MD

Publication date: 1921 in the manuscript *Psychodiagnostik*

What the test measures: Personality structure and dynamics, including cognitive, affective/emotional, ego functioning, defenses, conflicts, coping mechanisms

Age range: Primarily adult; normative data is also available for adolescents and children.

Administration time: The association portion requires from 10 to 15 minutes; the inquiry portion requires another 20 to 30 minutes; scoring and interpretation can take as long as 2 hours depending on the number and complexity of responses.

Qualification of examiners: Administration, scoring, and interpretation requires extensive training and practice.

Publisher: Verlag Hans Huber, Medical Publisher, Bern, Switzerland.
Distributed by The Psychological Corporation
555 Academic Court
San Antonio, TX 78204-2498
800-211-8378
10 Psychodiagnostic Plates, $119.50; package of 100 Structural Summary Blanks, $48.50; *The Rorschach: A Comprehensive System*, vols. 1 and 2, $98.00, vol. 3, $96.00 (all prices as of January 2000)
Also distributed by Western Psychological Services
For current ordering information
800-648-8857

administration and scoring. Volume one, in its second edition, focuses on interpretation, and volume two is devoted to the use of the Rorschach with children and adolescents. Another important reference is *A Rorschach Workbook for the Comprehensive System* (Exner, 1995). This book, published by Exner's Rorschach Workshops, provides the fundamentals of administration and scoring, descriptive statistics for various clinical and nonclinical groups, and some 300 responses to practice scoring.

🪶 TEST YOURSELF 🪶

1. **The inkblot procedure was originally used as a test to evaluate which of the following?**

   (a) personality dynamics

   (b) imagination

   (c) intelligence

   (d) visual perception

2. **The most significant contribution made by Exner to the evolution of the Rorschach was**

   (a) expanding the normative database.

   (b) developing a consistent scoring system.

   (c) standardizing administration procedures.

   (d) all of these.

3. **Consistent with the original intent of Hermann Rorschach, the philosophy and procedures of Exner's Comprehensive System focus on**

   (a) content interpretation.

   (b) response determinants.

   (c) only deviant or unusual responses.

   (d) response location.

4. **The test-retest reliability coefficients of the Rorschach show variability where expected. What type of subjects taking the test would tend to show the most variability in their Rorschach protocols over time?**

   (a) subjects with low intelligence

   (b) subjects who have children

   (c) children tested at different ages

   (d) ethnic minorities

5. **The number and type of Rorschach responses delivered by a subject can be affected by which of the following?**

   (a) intelligence

   (b) age

   (c) mood

   (d) any of these

continued

6. What is the primary purpose of the inquiry phase of administration?

(a) to clarify the subject's response

(b) to obtain additional responses from the subject

(c) to evaluate the subject's reactions to the inkblot

(d) to reduce the number of responses offered by the subject

7. The Structural Summary is used for all of the following except

(a) recording each response.

(b) interpreting response patterns.

(c) calculating ratios and percentages.

(d) tabulating response frequency.

Answers: 1. b; 2. d; 3. b; 4. c; 5. d; 6. a; 7. b

Two

HOW TO ADMINISTER THE RORSCHACH

Erica Wilson, Julie Reese, and Tara Rose

Administration is key to good assessment. Accurate scoring and meaningful interpretation of a test instrument, particularly the Rorschach, requires following the proper and correct procedures. Examiners who administer the Rorschach make important decisions throughout the administration process that significantly influence how the data will be scored. Familiarity with all aspects of Rorschach administration will ensure the most accurate assessment of the examinee's psychological functioning.

Rorschach administration consists of two distinct phases: Response and Inquiry. Both phases are designed to elicit valid and interpretable responses from the examinee to allow for answers to specific referral questions. Unofficially, a "preparation" or introduction phase of administration also exists, in which much of the groundwork is laid before the examinee walks into the testing room. This phase involves providing specific testing conditions (e.g., test environment, test materials, establishing rapport) that are critical to the generation and accurate recording of Rorschach responses.

WHEN SHOULD THE RORSCHACH BE USED?

Deciding to use the Rorschach is ultimately dependent on the clinical question that the examiner is trying to answer. It can be used alone or in conjunction with other psychological tests. The Rorschach is a flexible instrument because subsets of variables can be used to draw valid inferences about multiple domains of personality functioning. The Rorschach provides descriptions of coping styles, available resources for coping, stress tolerance, affective disturbance, ability to modulate emotion, problem-solving style, psychotic disturbance, reality testing, perceptual accuracy, interpersonal perceptions, self-perceptions, and personal issues (preoccupations, motivations, underlying needs). Based on these descriptions, the Rorschach can be helpful in therapy (e.g., to monitor change, reveal treatment issues), for differential diagnosis, and treatment planning (e.g., to identify preferred modes of coping and problem solving). Additionally, the Rorschach can assess how an examinee responds to an ambiguous situation.

APPROPRIATE TESTING CONDITIONS

Testing Environment

Although the ideal testing environment is a quiet, comfortable room that is free of distractions, examiners often must administer the Rorschach in less than optimal settings such as schools, hospitals, clinics, and prisons. In any kind of setting, the examiner works to create a testing situation that resembles the ideal as closely as possible. Most important is to find a place where only the examiner and examinee are present and others cannot interrupt. Interruptions can potentially interfere with the data by making the examinee feel nervous or awkward and possibly less motivated to become fully engaged in the test.

A table and two chairs offer the most comfortable seating arrangement; however a chair may be substituted for a table or the table eliminated completely and the cards placed on the examiner's lap. A clipboard aids the examiner in recording responses. It is standard administration procedure for the examiner to sit beside the examinee. It is also helpful to be slightly behind the examinee. *Do not sit face-to-face.* This seating arrangement prevents any subtle communication by the examiner to the examinee that may influence the examinee's responses. See Figure 2.1 for alternative seating arrangements.

Testing Materials

Rorschach Cards

The 10 Rorschach cards are the only materials that are presented to the examinee. It is important that the cards be stacked in numerical order, face down, with Card I on top. Then, as each card is turned over, it is presented to the examinee in the correct order, facing right side up.

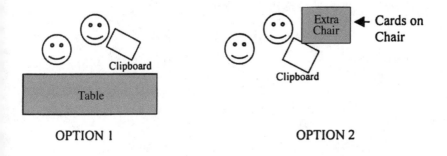

Figure 2.1 Alternative Seating Arrangements for Testing

Response Forms

There is no standard response form that accompanies the Rorschach, but there is a general format that is followed. A sample response form (in Appendix 1), created by the authors, may be reproduced and used to record Rorschach responses. This form makes it easy to record all of the information gathered during administration: the card number and position (v, <, >), the response, and the inquiry. This format is particularly helpful in organizing the responses, and it facilitates the writing of the responses verbatim.

The examiner will need at least 15 response forms (or sheets of paper) to record the examinee's responses. There are unusual cases where an examiner may use as many as 30 response forms because the examinee provides so many responses.

Location Sheet

There is a standardized Location sheet with 10 miniature reproductions of the inkblots, used to record what part of the inkblot is used in each response. The Location sheets are available separately in color or black and white. There is also a Location sheet on the Structural Summary Blank, a six-page form created for use with Exner's Comprehensive System. The Structural Summary Blank includes all the standardized forms needed for scoring, as well as a demographics page that can be filled out before testing begins.

DON'T FORGET 2.1

Keys for Preparing to Administer the Test

The Environment

- Quiet, distraction-free room
- Two chairs, side-by-side, examiner's chair slightly behind the examinee's chair (possibly an extra chair on which to place the cards)
- Table
- Room reserved for at least 90 minutes for adults, and 45 minutes for children

Examiner's Materials

- 10 Rorschach cards (face down, with Card I on top)
- Two or more pens or pencils
- 15 or more response forms (photocopied from Appendix 1)
- Location sheet
- Clipboard (response forms on top, location sheet underneath)
- Structural Summary Blank (includes the location sheet)
- Photocopied script from Appendix 2 and 3—optional
- Extra response forms (just in case)

During the administration of the Rorschach, it can be helpful for the examiner to use a clipboard, placing the Location sheet beneath the response forms to prevent the examinee from seeing it. Don't Forget Table 2.1 summarizes the preparation needed before testing begins.

Time Requirements

Do not rush through the Rorschach. The examiner should allot plenty of time for Rorschach administration in order to allow for accurate recording of responses and adequate inquiry of those responses. A typical administration lasts between 40 and 55 minutes, but the examiner should work at a comfortable pace. On average, 20 minutes are needed to complete the Response Phase and at least 30 minutes to complete the Inquiry Phase, depending on how cooperative and articulate the examinee may be. Naturally, additional time will be needed to go through the cards a second time if the examinee does not provide enough answers for a valid and interpretable protocol. Administration for children under the age of 10 varies slightly, averaging 60 minutes to complete a record.

TESTING INDIVDUALS WITH SPECIAL NEEDS

In testing individuals with special needs (e.g., hearing impairment or primary language other than English), the examiner needs to follow the standardized administration as closely as possible. If the examiner is working with an examinee whose primary language is different than his or her own, it is best to get another examiner who can speak the same language. If this is not possible, working with an interpreter is a viable option. The interpreter should be briefed on the need to say only what the examiner says and repeat only what the examinee says. The interpreter needs to be especially careful about not communicating any judgments about the content of the examinee's responses. Whenever an examinee's needs necessitate modifying in the administration, the examiner should include a description of those specific changes in the report.

Not all persons with special needs can be given the Rorschach. For example, a person who has a significant visual impairment may not be able to see the cards. Clinical judgment should be used to determine whether the accommodations needed for a person's special need will seriously impair the validity of the test. Caution 2.1 summarizes the modifications to standardized procedure.

CAUTION 2.1

Modifications to Standardized Procedure

- Changes made to accommodate an examinee's limitations should be done with caution and consideration of the validity of the results.
- Changes should always be noted in the report.
- When using an interpreter:
  1. It should be stressed that interpretation be done verbatim. Nothing in the interpretation should be added or subtracted from what is said by the examiner or examinee.
  2. The interpreter should be careful not to subtly communicate his or her reactions to the examinee's responses.

Testing Children

Although child assessment is not the focus of this book, the standard administration procedure should be followed as closely as possible when testing children. Briefly, establishing rapport is paramount to eliciting cooperation, calming anxieties, and obtaining valid test results. It is equally important to be sensitive to the overtesting of children, especially if the Rorschach is part of a larger test battery. For example, it is not desirable to administer a Rorschach immediately following a demanding task. The scheduling of a nontest activity (e.g., coloring, free play, conversation) is sometimes warranted between tests in a battery or the examiner should consider scheduling the testing across two or three sessions.

Furthermore, children may require more breaks than adults, given their shorter attention span and restlessness. It is acceptable in the testing environment if a child wants to stand up or sit on the floor. If a child is highly distractible or hyperactive, Rorschach administration may be considered inappropriate. Given these guidelines, the examiner should always use sound clinical judgment in determining how long and how well a child can respond to the Rorschach. Examiners should refer to Volume three of Exner's Comprehensive System books for testing children and adolescents (Exner, 1995).

RAPPORT WITH EXAMINEE

Helping the examinee to feel comfortable and at ease during the testing is crucial to good administration. The purpose of the Rorschach is to gather information about the psychological makeup of the examinee, so the manner in which the examiner prepares the examinee can increase an examinee's willingness to respond or, conversely, his or her anxiety and defensiveness. It is important to maintain a positive rapport throughout the testing session. Although idle conversation should be minimized, the interaction should be pleasant and comfortable. Because of the ambiguous nature of the Rorschach, examinees often have many questions. Knowing how to respond to each question in a manner that does not "guide" the responses will help the examiner keep the interpersonal interaction smooth and natural. Additionally, knowing how to transition from the Response Phase to the Inquiry Phase will help the examinee feel more at ease.

We offer you scripts for the administration of the Rorschach Introduction, Response, and Inquiry Phases. The script will help the first-time examiner with rapport as well as maintaining the standardized protocol. The script also offers possible answers to frequently asked questions. The Introduction and Response Phase script is in Appendix 2 and the Inquiry Phase script is in Appendix 3. You may photocopy the script and refer to it during administration.

Establishing Rapport

The best way to begin establishing rapport is to inquire about previous testing experiences by stating, **"One of the tests we will be doing is the inkblot test, the Rorschach. Have you ever heard of it, or have you ever taken it?"** The examinee's answer to this question will help reveal whether he or she has had any negative experiences related to assessment. If so, it will be important to be sensitive to the way in which the individual responds to the current testing situation. It may be necessary to spend more time discussing what made the previous experience unpleasant for the examinee and extend appropriate empathy toward his or her current feelings on testing. By asking about previous knowledge, experience, or impressions regarding the Rorschach, the examiner can correct any misperceptions as well as calm anxieties.

Providing a brief introduction to the test is also important in building rapport. An appropriate introduction explains how the Rorschach is clinically useful and what is expected of the examinee during the test. An examiner might say, **"It is a test that gives us some information about your personality, and by having that information we can . . . [plan your treatment easier; understand your problem a bit better; answer some of the questions you have about yourself more precisely; make some recommendations that your doctor has requested; get some idea about how your treatment program is progressing, etc.]"** The examiner can then futher explain the test by saying, **"I'm going to show you a series of inkblots and I want you to tell me what you think they look like."**

Maintaining Rapport

When testing begins, the examiner should avoid superfluous talk. However, the examiner should continue to try to respond to the examinee's questions in a natural and straightforward manner in order to provide a comfortable interpersonal situation. Common questions during the testing often relate to the examinee's concern about giving the correct response or to uncertainty about how the responses provide any relevant information for the examiner. The best way to re-

DON'T FORGET 2.2

Keys to Building and Maintaining Positive Examiner-Examinee Rapport

- Ask about previous testing experiences in order to address any negative impressions.
- Inquire about knowledge and perceptions regarding the Rorschach and seek to correct misunderstandings.
- Give a brief explanation of the Rorschach.
- If needed, take extra time in the beginning to calm examinee's anxieties or concerns.
- Respond to questions in a natural manner, yet limit the amount of information provided.
- Assure the examinee that the results will be fully explained in a follow-up session.

spond is to give as little information as possible while still addressing the question. For example, upon being asked *"What should I see?"* an examiner might say **"People see all kinds of things."** Such a response does not influence how the examinee will respond to the cards.

If an examinee says *"I don't see how you can get any information from these tests,"* the examiner could respond, **"It's better to wait to answer these questions until we have finished [all the testing, our work together, or the assessment]. I'll be sure to give you the results of the test at a later date."** This assures the examinee that the results will be provided without giving too much information about the Rorschach test itself. (For a list of responses to common questions see the scripts in Appendixes 2 and 3.)

Remember that while the examiner does not want to reveal a lot about the test, he or she does want to be sensitive and empathic toward the examinee's experience. If the examinee does seem extremely anxious, it is often best to take some time to find out the reasons for the anxiety. Taking an extra few minutes to talk calmly with an examinee is usually enough to ease anxiety and any concerns he or she may have. Don't Forget 2.2 summarizes key points in establishing rapport.

THE RESPONSE PHASE (ASSOCIATION PHASE)

The examiner is ready to begin the Response Phase after establishing rapport, explaining the purpose of the assessment, and giving proper instruction. One of the examiner's main goals of the Response Phase is to gather a sufficient number of responses that can later be coded and interpreted to provide a valid description of the examinee's psychological functioning. At the same time, the examinee's objective is to scan the blot, classify potential answers, discard or censor unwanted answers, select a potential answer, and articulate a response.

The Rorschach Cards

The 10 Rorschach cards are numbered on the back (I–X) and administered in numerical order beginning with Card I. The number on the backside should be on the top, right-hand corner. During the test, it is important to place the inkblots face-down in a discreet location where the examinee has a limited view of them. (The examinee must not see the actual inkblots before the examiner hands each one to him or her at the appropriate time.)

The Response Phase begins when the examiner turns over the first card, hands it to the examinee in the face-up position, and asks, *"What might this be?"* Once the examinee starts to respond, it is crucial that the examiner write down verbatim what is said, even if it seems irrelevant. Sometimes, seemingly irrelevant words add to the coding by providing determinants or special scores or, at the very least, can be a part of the behavioral observations. If an examinee is speaking too quickly or the examiner misses something that is said, it is acceptable to ask the examinee to slow down and repeat him- or herself by saying, **"Please wait, I'm having trouble keeping up with you,"** or **"Go a little slower please,"** or **"I'm sorry, I didn't get all of that,"** **"You said two people with hats and . . . ?"** The examinee will likely indicate when he or she is done by handing the card back to the examiner or pausing to wait for the examiner to continue.

The Appropriate Use of Encouragement

Obtaining an adequate and reasonable number of responses to allow for a usable protocol can be enhanced by the use of encouragement. On Card I, the examinee must provide more than one response. If the examinee appears to be done or hands the card to the examiner after only one response, the examiner may encourage further responses by saying, **"Most people see more than one thing"** and then provide time for additional responses. If the examinee does not or is unable to respond, then the examiner can offer more encouragement by saying, **"Take your time, I'm sure you can see more."** When an examinee asks about what he or she should see, how many responses she or he should give, or if he or she can turn the cards, the examiner may reply, **"Just tell me**

CAUTION 2.2

Common Mistakes in Administration

- Forgetting to put the cards in order
- Sitting face-to-face
- Forgetting to get more than one response on the first card
- Forgetting to intervene after five responses on the first card or whenever the examinee first provides five responses
- Forgetting to go back through the cards if less than 14 responses are given
- Letting the examinee see the blots before they are presented

---

what you see there" or "It's up to you" or "Most people find more than one thing" or "People see all kinds of things." When no response is given and an examinee appears to be having trouble, an examiner may encourage the examinee by saying, "Take your time. We're in no hurry. Everyone can find something." Even with encouraging words and patience, an examinee may not provide 14 or more responses after finishing Card X. In this case, a protocol of less than 14 cannot be coded and the examiner must start the process over beginning with Card I. The examiner encourages the examinee to continue by saying, "Now you know how it's done, but there's a problem. You didn't give me enough responses. So, we're going to go back through the cards again. You can use the same responses as before but this time I want you to give me more responses. OK?" The Rorschach is then administered in the same manner as before, beginning with Card I.

In contrast, when an examinee starts off by giving five responses to Card I and appears to be continuing, the examiner should take the card and say, "Alright, let's do the next one." If the examinee tries to give more than five responses to Card II then the same procedure should be used. If at any time after Card II the examinee gives only five responses and stops voluntarily, this procedure should be discontinued. Caution 2.2 outlines common pitfalls in administering the Rorschach.

Recording Responses

From the moment the examinee begins to respond to what he or she sees in the inkblot, the examiner should be transcribing the response. Recording responses accurately is an important aspect to coding and interpreting of the Rorschach. The standardized protocol calls for using a landscape or horizontal format on $8\frac{1}{2}$ by 11-inch paper with columns to record information.

Rapid Reference 2.1

Common Abbreviations for Recording Responses

a animal	ex explosion	na nature
abt about	et everything	o oh
at anything	fd food	r are
b be	frt front	sc science
bec because	fi fire	ss some sort
bf butterfly	g gee	st something
bl blood	ge geography	sx sex
c see	hh household	u you
cb could be	j just	wm woman
cg clothing	ll looks like	xy x -ray
cl cloud	ls landscape	y why
dk don't know	mayb may be	-g ing

Note. Exner, J. E. (1993). *The Rorschach: A Comprehensive System*, Volume 1

The card number is written in the left column (e.g., I, II, III), followed by the number of the response (e.g., 1, 2, 3) in the next column. (When starting a new page, it is essential to enter the response number because it will help determine if the examinee has given enough total responses at the end of the administration.) Responses are numbered consecutively beginning with Card I and continuing through Card X. For example, if an examinee gives three responses for Card I, then the first response on Card II is number four.

The next two columns are for the Response and Inquiry. Under the Response column, the examiner first notes if the orientation of the card for the response is not in standard position (e.g., the examinee has turned the card) by using a caret mark. The vertex of the caret indicates the position of the top of the card during the response: top to the left (<), top to the right (>), inverted (V), and fully rotated card (o). No caret mark is used when the examinee keeps the card in its standard position.

After the position of the card has been noted, the examiner writes *verbatim* what the examinee says. Every word and phrase may later be important to the interpretation. The use of abbreviations makes this an easier task. Rapid Reference 2.1 provides commonly used abbreviations. The use of Exner's abbreviations is recommended in the event that the actual test data need to be referred to by an-

Table 2.1   Format for Recording Responses

Card	Resp. #	Free Association	Inquiry
I.	1	A wolf face, yeah, a wolf face. See here, the eyes	E: Rpts. S: Yes, see the eyes here and here are the ears. This is the shape of a wolf face. E: What makes it ll eyes? S: Because they're white
	2	> This little part ll a dog's nose and ears, kind a like a profile of a dog's face.	E: Repeats S: Yeah, see this part is shaped this big, like an ear and this part here is the snout. E: Profile? S: Just because I only see an ear and the side of the nose. Pts.
II.	3	These ll dancg bears	E: Repeats S: Yeah, see how they're like dancg with each other E: What makes them ll dancg bears? S: You can see the body ll bears on their legs and the way they are facg each other makes it ll they are dancg.

other professional. Remember that when needed, it is permissible to ask the examinee to slow down. Leave ample space between responses to allow for the recording of the Inquiry. Some first-time Rorschach examiners use a separate response sheet for each response or put only two responses on each page.

The Inquiry is recorded in the far right column on the response sheet. Using "E" for examiner and "S" for subject (examinee), the dialogue (titled "Inquiry") is recorded. At the same time, for each response the examiner also circles the area used by the examinee for the response on the Location sheet. The process of scoring is made easier by clearly circling the location, numbering the location, and identifying several details of the response on the Location sheet. Provided is an example of three responses, both how they are recorded on the response sheet, and how the cards are labeled on the Location sheet. Table 2.1 illustrates the format for recording Rorschach responses and Figure 2.2 is the sample Location sheet.

Recording Behavioral Observations

An examinee's behaviors and gestures are recorded as well as his or her verbal responses to the inkblots. For example, frequent shifting in one's chair, cry-

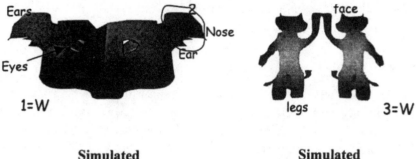

Figure 2.2 Example of Location Sheet

Note: Sample, NOT an actual Rorschach inkblot

ing, shaky hands, or raising one's voice can be written in the margin of the response sheet. These observations provide additional clinical information about an examinee's response to the examiner, the testing situation, and collateral data about an examinee's response to a particular card.

INQUIRY PHASE

The final phase of administration is the Inquiry Phase, in which the major goal is to gather additional information from the examinee to ensure that the coding of each response is as accurate as possible. During the Inquiry, the examiner tries to understand the examinee's response as it occurred during the Response Phase, including seeing what the examinee perceived, its location on the inkblot, and the features or determinants used to generate that particular response.

The Link between the Inquiry and Coding

Most responses cannot be accurately coded before gathering additional information during the Inquiry. A full understanding of the three elements of coding — content (what is it), location (where is it), and determinants (what makes it look like that) — guide the Inquiry so that the responses can be correctly coded. On occasion, an examinee may offer a response that contains all three elements of the coding without additional inquiry. For example, a response such as "The whole thing [location] looks like a bat [content], because it is black [color determinant] and because of the shape [form determinant] of its wings and body" provides all the elements for accurate coding. However, this occurs so rarely, that every response usually needs to be queried.

Method of Inquiry

The Inquiry begins after the examinee's last response to the final card (Card X). The examiner arranges the cards so that they are in order, face-down, with Card I on top and placed as they were during the Response Phase. The examiner transitions from the Response Phase to the Inquiry Phase by saying, **"Okay, now we've done them all. We are going to go back through the cards again. It won't take very long. I want to see the things that you said you saw and make sure that I see them like you do. We'll do them one at a time. I'll read what you said and then I want you to show me where it is in the blot and then tell me what is there that makes it look like that, so I can see it too, just like you did. Is that clear?"** After instruction, an examinee may still have questions. The following are commonly asked questions and acceptable examiner responses.

> Examinee: *Why do I have to do this?*
> Examiner: **So I can see things that you saw.**
> Examinee: *What do you want me to tell you?*
> Examiner: **Just show me where you saw it and what makes it look like that.**
> Examinee: *Should I find other things too?*
> Examiner: **No, I'm only interested in the things you saw before.**

When the examinee understands what is expected, the examiner proceeds by handing Card I to the examinee and reading the response **"Here you said . . ."** one at a time, allowing the examinee to explain further, and then recording the examinee's answers to the Inquiry questions. The examiner is always mindful of the goal of the Inquiry: to obtain the three coding elements of content, location, and determinants (see Don't Forget 2.3). (First-time examiners, the next chapter provides the coding definitions, which are important to review before administering your first Rorschach.) If an examinee does not spontaneously provide enough information or if coding elements remain unclear, the examiner follows up with additional questions, being careful not to lead the examinee's responses.

The coding element of content is usually evident in the response itself; however, to clarify location, the examiner may say, **" I don't think I see it cor-**

rectly. **Run your finger around it or show me where it is."** Obtaining determinants can be the most challenging because an examinee may not clearly state the features (e.g., color, shape, shading, movement) of the inkblot used in forming his or her perception. An object may be perceived in a inkblot because of its color, shape, movement,

> **DON'T FORGET 2.3**
>
> **Three Coding Elements to Remember during Inquiry**
> - Content (what is it)
> - Location (where is it)
> - Determinants (what makes it look like that)

or any combination of features. To clarify, an examiner may say, **"I'm not sure what there is that makes it look like that"** or **"Help me to see it the way that you did."** The examinee's words are coded; therefore, if a coding element (usually a Determinant) is not clearly stated or reasonably conveyed through the examinee's description, it cannot be scored. The examiner *never* provides examples of possible determinants to the examinee.

Resistance on the part of the examinee can complicate the Inquiry Phase. An examinee's resistance may take the form of *"I didn't say that"* or *"I don't know why, it just looks like that to me"* or *"I can't see it."* An examiner should respond in a firm and tactful manner: **"Come on now. Look, I wrote it down. You can find it, take your time"** or **"We are in no hurry. You found it once, I'm sure you can find it again"** or **"I know it looks like that to you, but remember I need to see it, too. So help me. Tell me about some of the things you see there that make it look like [a mask, a bat, etc.]."**

Keys Words

Key words are typically adjectives (e.g., shiny, lovely, huge) and sometimes nouns (e.g., circus, fair, carnival) that are given by the examinee either in the Response or Inquiry Phase that imply a determinant (i.e., features of the inkblot that have not been explicitly stated by the examinee). For this reason, key words suggest further inquiry (see Don't Forget 2.4). Consider the key words in the following responses:

1. "This is a lovely, blooming flower."
2. "I think that's a circus full of animals and acrobats."
3. "That is a monster with huge feet wearing a slick coat."

In sentence 1, *lovely* and *blooming* give additional information about the flower that goes beyond the obvious shape of the inkblot. *Lovely* may imply the use of color or merely shape. To clarify this response, an examiner can query the key word *lovely* by saying, **"You mentioned it's lovely"** or **"I'm not sure what makes it lovely"** or **"What is there about it that makes it look lovely?"** Likewise, *blooming* may imply movement of the flower or the use of shading to describe the different positions of the petals. In sentence 2, the word *circus* is more complex because it may imply a combination of the inkblot's features, such as color and movement. *Huge* and *slick* in sentence 3 may imply dimension, shape, or texture. Key words should always be queried in a nondirective manner as described in the query of sentence 1.

Inappropriate questions

Direct questions, leading questions, or questions that are not relevant to coding should never be asked during the Inquiry. Examples of these kinds of questions are

> "Was it the shape?"
> "Did the color help?"
> "Would it look like that if it were bigger?"
> "Is there anything else you can tell me about that?"
> "Are they males or females?"

Examiners may be tempted to ask these questions if a suspected determinant has not yet been revealed by the examinee or if the examiner finds a question clinically interesting. Questions of this nature, however, can compromise the validity of the Rorschach protocol. Caution 2.3 highlights common pitfalls to avoid in the Inquiry Phase of administration.

TESTING LIMITS

The testing of limits is not a part of the typical Rorschach administration and should be used with caution. The testing of limits occurs after the Inquiry when the examiner asks additional questions that are not used in the coding of the response. Typically, an examiner will choose 2 to 3 inkblots (e.g., Cards III, VIII, and possibly V) to which the examinee has not given the popular response and says, **"Sometimes people see a [a bat, human figure, etc.] There, do you see anything that looks like that?"** This procedure is most useful when no or very few (1 to 2) popular responses are given, or when the examiner is trying to differentiate between individuals who have significant perceptual distortions and individuals who are perceptually intact but choose to discard obvious answers for more creative, idiosyncratic responses. This is an optional procedure that should be used only when there is some specific benefit that outweighs the risk of contaminating future administrations of the Rorschach. When an examinee is asked if he or she can see [a bat, human figure, etc.], the examiner communicates an expectation of what the examinee is supposed to see. If the examinee is tested again, he or she may give a popular response the examiner mentioned, thus reducing the accuracy of the Rorschach. First-time administrators may want to discuss testing limits with their supervisors before actually using the procedure with an examinee. Rapid Reference 2.2 describes testing limits of the Rorschach.

CAUTION 2.3

Common Mistakes in the Inquiry

- Hurrying through the inquiry
- Not clearly understanding the location or determinants used
- Forgetting to inquire key words (adjectives, complex nouns)
- Not writing verbatim what was said
- Asking leading questions (for example, if the examinee says, "They are so beautiful" and the examiner responds, "Because of the color?")

Rapid Reference 2.2

Testing Limits

- Testing limits are used when examinees give no or few popular responses.
- To test limits, the examiner goes back through cards after test administration and asks examinee if he or she sees popular responses.
- Examiners must be careful when testing limits because it influences future Rorschach administrations.

🗝 TEST YOURSELF 🗝

1. **In addition to the Rorschach cards, what does the examiner need to administer the test?**

2. **When giving the Rorschach cards, the examiner should**
   (a) sit face-to-face and ask the examinee to imagine what is on the card.
   (b) sit face-to-face and ask "What might this be?"
   (c) sit side-by-side and ask the examinee to imagine what he or she sees.
   (d) sit side-by-side and ask "What might this be?"

3. **If less than 14 responses are given in Response Phase, what should the examiner do?**

4. **What parts of an examinee's response are of particular interest in the Inquiry Phase?**
   (a) adjectives
   (b) complex nouns
   (c) anything the examiner is unsure about
   (d) all of the above

5. **The examiner is free to use any personal abbreviations he or she chooses because only the examiner needs to read what is written.** True or False?

6. **Why is it important to write verbatim what the examinee says?**

7. **Which of the following is a leading Inquiry question?**
   (a) "I'm not sure I see it as you do. Can you help me understand why it looks like that?"
   (b) "Does the color make it look like that?"
   (c) "What makes it look like an ocean?"
   (d) "You said 'lovely'?"

8. **The behavioral observations are not important because they are not part of the scoring system and have no role in the interpretation.** True or False?

9. **It is important to get a complete protocol, with 14 or more responses, whether or not the examinee seems anxious, or angry.** True or False?

10. **What is the purpose of the Inquiry?**

Answers: 1. several pens or pencils, 15-plus response sheets, location sheet, clipboard, script sheet (optional); 2. d; 3. Say "Now you know how it's done. But you didn't give me enough responses. So we're going to go back through the cards again. You can use the same responses as before, but this time I want you to give me more responses. OK?" Then the examiner proceeds with Card I exactly like the first administration; 4. d; 5. False. It is important to use standardized abbreviations so that others can review the response at a later date; 6. Because each word is important in the interpretation. Even the words that are not directly answering a response provide information about the examinee's approach to the test (anxiety level, thought processes etc.); 7. b; 8. False. Behavioral observations are an important component of any psychological report; 9. False. There are many components to validity—It is important to get a complete protocol; but pushing a resistant examinee may not generate a more useful Rorschach protocol. 10. The purpose of the Inquiry is to obtain enough data to be able to code the protocol.

Three

HOW TO CODE THE RORSCHACH

Tara Rose

Coding Rorschach responses is an involved process. It requires taking all of the text transcribed during the test administration (qualitative material) and turning it into numeric scores (quantitative information) that will later be used in the structural summary, and ultimately, for interpretation.

There are two parts to the coding process. The first involves coding each response and the second involves entering the codes (or scores) for each response onto a page that organizes all the coded information category by category, called the Sequence of Scores sheet. (The codes can also be entered into a computer program such as RIAP or ROR-SCAN that can generate the Sequence of Scores sheet.) We will walk you through each task, step-by-step.

Once the examiner has completed the two steps outlined in this chapter, he or she will then tally the coded information and compute the summary scores and indices for the Structural Summary. Creating the Structural Summary is discussed in detail in the next chapter.

THE CODING PROCESS

Coding responses is probably the most difficult task for the new examiner. Learning to accurately code the Rorschach takes time and requires guidance from an experienced examiner or Rorschacher. We strongly recommend that any examiner who plans to use the Rorschach take a class and/or be supervised by someone with experience in administering the Rorschach.

Before discussing the actual coding system, two important aspects of the Rorschach coding process need to be emphasized. First, the examiner must understand the theoretical goal behind Rorschach coding. Second, the examiner must rely on the coding rules in Exner's *Comprehensive System* (vol. 1, 1993) in order to accurately score the responses. As a complement, we have created a Rorschach Scoring worksheet (see Appendix 4) that helps with speed and accuracy in coding, which the first-time examiner may find useful.

Theoretical Goals Underlying the Coding Process

Understanding the theory behind the Rorschach is helpful to the coding process. An experienced examiner makes final decisions based on the theoretical framework of the test and the coding process. Read chapter 2 from Exner's *Comprehensive System* (vol. 1, 1993) for a more complete understanding of the Rorschach. Essentially, this broad-reaching test is composed of a stimulus that allows the examinee's traits and styles to be expressed. When interpreting the data, the examiner cannot focus solely on one small aspect of the examinee or one small coded variable; each aspect can be understood only in the context of the examinee's other features. A whole picture of the examinee must be developed, a task that can challenge a new or inexperienced examiner.

The overarching goal of coding is to try to understand "how the characteristics of a person merge together in a series of complex interrelationships that breeds a reasonable understanding of that person" through the protocol (Exner, 1993, p. 85). Futhermore, the cardinal rule in coding Rorschach responses is that "the code or score should represent the cognitive operation at the time the subject gave the answer" (p. 85). Don't code the response that first appears during the Inquiry Phase; to code accurately, you must include data from both the Response and Inquiry. However, "The coder-interpreter must resist the temptation to consider the original response and the information developed in the Inquiry as being continuous, for this is an illogical assumption. Many events transpire between the original response and the Inquiry and . . . the latter occurs under a much different structure than the former" (Exner, 1993, p. 87). In other words, the examinee's experience may differ between Response and Inquiry Phase. The examiner must note the difference.

The second most important rule in the coding process is that "all of the components that appear in the response should appear in the coding" (Exner, 1993, p. 87). In other words, don't leave anything out that should have been coded. Errors of omission are often much more important than coding disagreements because they can lead to a distorted picture of the examinee's

≡ Rapid Reference 3.1

Coding Rules

- Overarching goal of the coding process: to understand "how the characteristics of a person merge together in a series of complex interrelationships that breeds a reasonable understanding of that person" (Exner, 1993, p. 85).
- Cardinal rule of coding: "The code or score should represent the cognitive operation at the time the subject gave the answer" (Exner, 1993, p. 85).
- Second rule of coding: "All of the components that appear in the response should appear in the coding" (Exner, 1993, p. 87). Avoid errors of omission.

psychological characteristics. Rapid Reference 3.1 summarizes the Rorschach (Exner, 1993) coding rules.

What Needs to Be Coded?

Every one of the examinee's responses to the inkblots must be coded under multiple categories. In order to accurately code each response, an examiner relies on a codebook that lists the rules on how to categorize qualitative information (in this case the examinee's responses to the inkblot). The codebook allows any trained examiner to code responses reliably.

That codebook for the Rorschach inkblot test can be found in Chapters 4 through 9 of Exner's *Comprehensive System* (vol. 1, 1993). Exner's Workbook (1995), while more accessible, simply does not cover all the information needed to accurately code the responses. This Essentials guide also does not cover all the rules of the coding system (see Caution 3.1) and is not meant to replace Volume 1 or the Workbook. Instead, it should be viewed as a companion to Volume 1, providing an overview of the coding system. As a guide it also provides lists of general rules and scoring descriptions.

CAUTION 3.1

The Examiner's Primary Source for Coding

To code completely and accurately, rely on the The Rorschach: A Comprehensive System, (vol. 1, Exner, 1993).

Our Rorschach Scoring Worksheet: Accuracy, Speed, Confidence

Our Rorschach Scoring worksheet, located in Appendix 4, will help first-time examiners code as accurately, completely, and quickly as possible. It also allows examiners to use Exner's preferred continuous approach to coding. A continuous approach coding strategy involves taking a single response and going through each of the coding categories for that response before starting the scoring process for the next response. Scoring in this manner allows the examiner to think in terms of the integrated score and helps to avoid errors of addition and omission.

The Rorschach Scoring worksheet helps the examiner thoroughly cover all coding categories for each response by providing a separate worksheet for each response (see Rapid Reference 3.2). The worksheet includes the seven coding categories, special directions, references to the coding rules in Volume 1 of Exner's Comprehensive System book and his Workbook (1993, 1995), options for coding each category, and a space for coding justification.

Rapid Reference 3.3 describes how to use the Scoring worksheet in Appendix 4. The worksheet adds an extra step to Exner's Structural Summary, so it may appear to add time to the process. But in fact, it is a time saver because the examiner is less likely to be hesitant and more likely to code a response correctly and therefore feel more confident filling out the Sequence of Scores sheet. The worksheet is most useful for the first few administrations, when the new user is most unfamiliar with the complex coding process. Examiners may attempt to expedite coding by omitting the basis for a coding decision. However, including the information will make it much easier to explain the reasoning in class or supervision.

STEP-BY-STEP CODING

While it is true that the Rorschach is a sophisticated and complex coding system, the examiner should also know that in many ways it is very clear-cut and manageable. There are seven steps for coding each response since there are seven categories to code: (1) Location and Developmental Quality, (2) Determinants, (3) Form Quality, (4) Contents, (5) Popular Responses, (6) Organizational Activity (Z score),

---

≡ *Rapid Reference 3.2*

Highlights of the Rorschach Scoring Worksheet

- There are separate sections for coding each of the seven categories.
- Sections parallel the Structural Summary sheet.
- Special directions for coding are given in "( )"s.
- Scoring options within a category are given in "{ }"s.
- Reference pages to Exner's volume I book and workbook are given in "[ ]"s.

≡ Rapid Reference 3.3

Using the Scoring Worksheet in Appendix 4

1. Use one Scoring Worksheet for each response.
2. Fill in each coding category with a score or check the not applicable (n/a) box.
3. After entering a score, at the end of that row write in why you made the coding decision.
4. When coding is completed, transfer the codes onto the Sequence of Scores sheet or into a Rorschach computer program (discussed later in this chapter).

and (7) Special Scores (see Rapid Reference 3.4). Don't Forget 3.1 provides an easy way to remember the seven categories.

1) Location and Developmental Quality

Location

- Location refers to the section or area of the inkblot being used, with four possible symbols ranging from the whole inkblot to an unusual detail (see Table 3.1).
- The scoring goal is to determine what part of the inkblot was used in the response.

- Location captures how the person approached the inkblot.
- There are two parts to identify: the location code ($W, D, Dd,$ and S) and the location number (blank, 1–99).

≡ Rapid Reference 3.4

Seven Coding Categories

1. Location and Developmental Quality
2. Determinants
3. Form Quality
4. Contents
5. Popular Responses
6. Organizational Activity (Z score)
7. Special Scores

How to Code Location

- Use the location sheet to determine the outline of the inkblot. (The location sheet is the page with 10 miniature inkblots, available either as a separate page or as part of the Structural Summary Blank.)
- If the whole inkblot was used, code a W for location and leave the location number blank or insert a dash. W's do not have location numbers.

DON'T FORGET 3.1

Silly Sentences to Help Remember the Seven Categories

• Susie wanted to **locate and/or develop** an important **determinant** of what makes a **quality** life **forum.** For **contents,** she looked to **popular** magazines hoping to **organize** her thoughts and come up with a project that would get her a **special score** on the assignment.

• The student began her homework assignment. She wrote, "It's time for science to **locate and develop** the important **determinants** of what makes a life **form of quality."** Her **contents** of life theory might be **popular** someday. The teacher thought the paper needed some **organizational** help, but it got a **special score** for creativity.

• If a single portion or portions of the inkblot were used, the examiner will find the location codes and location numbers in Table A starting on page 195 of Volume 1 of Exner's *Comprehensive System,* 1993). Use Figures 7 through 16 within Table A (one table for each of the the ten cards) to determine the score.

  • First, determine if the portion(s) is a common detail response or an unusual detail response. If so, code *D* or *Dd.*

  • Second, determine if white space was used in the response. If so, the location code also includes an *S* after the *W, D,* or *Dd.*

  • Third, compare the part of the inkblot used with Table A and determine the location number. If the exact area is not listed, the location number is *99* (Example: *Dd27, D7,* or *Dd99*).

Rapid Reference 3.5 outlines rules for coding location with multiple *D* or *Dd* areas.

⎯ Rapid Reference 3.5

Rules for Multiple *D* and/or *Dd* Areas

1. Two or more combined *D* areas, code *D*

2. Two separate objects are both *D,* code *D*

3. Composite of two *D* areas, but uncommon response, code *Dd*

4. Two or more combined areas and at least two objects, code *Dd*

Table 3.1   Location of Responses

Symbol	Symbol Name	Explanation
W	Whole Response	• The entire inkblot. *All* portions of the inkblot *must* be used. No segment can be omitted.
D	Common Detail Response	• A frequently identified area of the inkblot. Area is included in Table A.
		• Two or more *D* areas used in one response that are listed in Table A.
Dd	Unusual Detail Response	• An infrequently identified area of the inkblot.
		• Two or more areas of the inkblot used in one response, with at least one area listed as *Dd* and/or not found at all in Table A. If area is not included in Table A, coding is *Dd* and location is *99 (Dd99)*.
S	Space Response	• White space area used in response, as well as *W, D,* and *Dd*.
		• Remember Space (*S*) is *never* scored alone, but as *WS, DS,* or *DdS*.

Note. Modified table from *The Rorschach: A Comprehensive System.* Volume 1: *Basic Foundations,* 3rd ed. (p. 94) by J. E. Exner, Jr., 1993, New York: John Wiley & Sons, Inc. Copyright 1993 by John Exner, Jr. Reprinted with permission.

Developmental Quality

- Developmental quality refers to the degree of meaningful organization or integration used in the response, with four possible symbols ranging from a synthesized to a vague response (see Table 3.2).
- The coding goal is to determine the quality of the processing of the response based on how form is used in the response.

How to Code Developmental Quality

- Refer to the location sheet to determine which portions of the inkblot are used.

Table 3.2   Developmental Quality

Symbol	Symbol Name	Explanation
+	Synthesized Response	• One or more objects are described as separate but related through position or movement. At least one of the objects must have a specific form demand or be described in a manner that creates a specific form demand.
		♦ Example: "Bird flying in a cloud" or "Two birds sitting on telephone wire."
v/+	Synthesized Response	• Two or more objects are described as separate but related. None of the objects have a specific form, and the description during inquiry does not introduce a form demand.
		♦ Example: "Two clouds coming together."
o	Ordinary Response	• A single object is described from an area of the inkblot, and the description creates a specific form demand. The object has features that emphasize its outline and structural features.
		• Two objects are described with no meaningful relationship between them.
		♦ Example: "One bird" or "Two birds."
v	Vague Response	• One or more unrelated objects are described without a specific form demand, outline, or structural features.
		♦ Example: "One cloud" or "Two clouds."

Note. Modified table from *The Rorschach: A Comprehensive System.* Volume 1: *Basic Foundations,* 3rd ed. (p. 99), by J. E. Exner, Jr., 1993, New York: John Wiley & Sons, Inc. Copyright 1993 by John Exner, Jr. Reprinted with permission.

- Determine developmental quality based on coding rules taking into consideration the number of objects and specific form demand (see Don't Forget box 3.2). Record only one code per response.

2) Determinants

- Determinants refers to the features, style, characteristics, or aspect of the inkblot that the examinee responded to, with 26 possible symbols from form to reflection responses (see Table 3.3).

- The scoring goal is "to provide information concerning the complex perceptual-cognitive process that has produced the response" (Exner, 1993, p. 103). Did the examinee respond to form, movement, color, shading, or symmetry of the inkblot?

- A blend is when more than one determinant is coded for a single (usually complex) response. A period (".") or full stop is placed between each determinant. Rapid Reference 3.6 describes the correct procedure for coding a blend.

- Some examiners and researchers consider determinants to be the most important aspect of the Rorschach to score, with the greatest implication for interpretation.

Table 3.3   Determinants

Symbol Name	Symbol	Explanation
Form	F	• Using *only* the form or shape features of the inkblot. No movement involved and rarely seen in blends.
Movement		• Movement (human, animal, or inanimate) used in the inkblot; movement is defined as any state of muscular tension.
	M (Human Movement Response)	• Responses with human activity. • Animal or a fictional character in a humanlike activity. • Animal movement where the movement describes a human activity that is *not* specific to that species. • Human experience such as emotion.
	FM (Animal Movement Response)	• Responses that include movement of an animal. Must be specific to the movements of that species of animal.
	m (Inanimate Movement Response)	• Responses with movement of an inanimate, inorganic, or dead object; may be static movement or an activity that is congruent with object.
Chromatic Color		• Using chromatic colors (colors of the rainbow, such as red, orange, yellow, green, blue, or violet) in the inkblot. *Not* black or white.
	C (Pure Color Response)	• Responses using *only* the chromatic colors with no form aspect reported.
	CF (Color Form Response)	• Responses primarily based on chromatic colors. Aspects of form are also included but are of secondary importance in the response.

Table 3.3   continued

Symbol Name	Symbol	Explanation
	FC (Form-Color Response)	• Responses based mainly on features of the form. Colors of the rainbow are included but are of secondary importance in the response and are used more as an elaboration and/or clarification.
	Cn (Color Naming Response)	• The chromatic colors of the inkblot are identified by name, such as "this is red, yellow, and blue."
Achromatic Color		• Using light and dark features of the inkblot, such as black, white, and gray features.
	C' (Pure Achromatic Color Response)	• Responses using *only* black, white, and gray features of the inkblot. Definitely viewed by examinee as color and no form is involved, such as "it's all black like at night."
	C'F (Achromatic Color-Form Response)	• Responses primarily based on black, white, and gray. Aspects of form are also included but are of secondary importance in the response.
	FC' (Form-Achromatic Color Response)	• Responses based mainly on features of the form. Black, white, and gray are included secondarily in the response and are more of an elaboration and/or clarification.
Shading-Texture		• Using light and dark features of the inkblot to suggest texture, such as *rough* or *furry*.
	T (Pure Texture Response)	• Shading components of the inkblot used to suggest texture or tactile qualities.
	TF (Texture-Form Response)	• Responses with the shading components interpreted as texture or tactile. Aspects of form are also included but are of secondary importance and are used for elaboration and/or clarification.

Table 3.3   continued

Symbol Name	Symbol	Explanation
	FT (Form-Texture Response)	• Responses based mainly on form features. Shading components of the inkblot used to suggest tactile qualities are included but are of secondary importance in the response.
Shading-Dimension		◆ Using shading to suggest a three-dimensional perspective.
	V (Pure Vista Response)	• Responses using shading components of the inkblot to suggest depth or dimensionality without form.
	VF (Vista-Form Response)	• The shading components are interpreted as depth or dimensionality. Aspects of form are included but are of secondary importance in the response.
	FV (Form-Vista Response)	• Responses based mainly on form features. Shading components of the inkblot are included to suggest dimensionality but are of secondary importance in the response.
Shading-Diffuse		◆ Using the diffuse shading of the inkblot, such as lighter and darker contrasts with no reference to either texture or dimension.
	Y (Pure Shading Response)	• Responses using *only* light-dark features of the inkblot without using form and with no reference to either texture or dimension.
	YF (Shading-Form Response)	• Responses primarily based on light-dark features of the inkblot. Aspects of form are also included but are of secondary importance in the response.
	FY (Form-Shading Response)	• Responses based mainly on features of the form. Light-dark features of the inkblot are included but are of secondary importance in the response.

Table 3.3   continued

Symbol Name	Symbol	Explanation
Form Dimension	FD (Form-Based Dimensional Response)	• Responses using three-dimensionality (3-D) based *only* on the form. Using elements of size and/or the shape of the outline in contrast to other areas of the inkblot; an object appearing in perspective or in relation to another object, such as a dog *in front of* or *behind* a tree. No use of shading is involved.
Pairs and Reflections		• Using two identical objects or percepts, either as a pair or reflection.
	2 (Pair Response)	• Responses using two identical images based on the symmetry of the inkblot. *Only* the objects in the response must be equivalent, not the entire inkblot. The objects must not be identified as being reflected or as mirror images.
	rF (Reflection-Form Response)	• Responses that include a reflection or a mirror image. The object or content has no specific form requirement such as clouds, landscape, and shadows.
	Fr (Form-Reflection Response)	• Responses that include reflection or a mirror image based on the symmetry of the inkblot. The response is based on form features and the object has a specific form.

Note. Modified table from *The Rorschach: A Comprehensive System.* Volume 1: *Basic Foundations,* 3rd ed. (pp. 104–5), by J. E. Exner, Jr., 1993, New York: John Wiley & Sons, Inc. Copyright 1993 by John Exner, Jr. Reprinted with permission.

≡ Rapid Reference 3.7

Form Rules

- *Form only:* If only form or shape is described, code form (*F*).
- *Form with movement:* If form is described with movement, code movement (*M, FM, m*).
- *Form dominant:* If form is the main determinant factor, elaborated by another aspect, code form first (*FC, FC', FT, FY, Fr*).
- *Form secondary:* If form is only modestly described, more as an elaboration to another aspect, code form second (*CF, C'F, TF, VF, YF, rF*).
- *Formless:* No form is described, code no form (*C, C', T, V, Y*).
- *Formless with Form:* Use a step-down rule. If a formless object is put in relation to an object with a form, then code form second (i.e., "Blood on a bear's body" steps down from a *C* for blood to a *CF*.
- *Reflections:* Reflection always includes some aspect of form, either primary or secondary (*Fr* or *rF*).

How to Score Determinants

- Rely on the transcribed text of the test and the description of what area of the inkblot was used (on the location sheet) to identify determinants.
- More than one determinant can be coded, but the same determinant cannot be coded twice for a single response.
- Form (*F*) is usually coded alone and it is extremely unusual to find in blends.
- If movement (*M, FM, m*) is used, a second code must be included to describe the movement as active, passive, or both. (See Table 3.4.)
- Active/passive codes are placed as superscripts after the movement determinant (i.e., M^p).

Rapid Reference 3.7 summarizes the form rules for coding the Rorschach.

Form Quality

- Form quality refers to how well an examinee's description of a form fits the area of the inkblot used, with four possible symbols from superior-overelaborated to minus (see Table 3.5).

Table 3.4 Active-Passive Movements

Movement Superscripts		◆ Any movement can be active, passive, or both.
	a (active)	• Responses with movement that is more dynamic or animated than *talking*. Examples in Table 11, page 110 of Exner (1993).
		• Responses in which an object is described as having both active and passive movements (i.e., a man leaning against a tree [passive] and tapping his foot [active]).
	p (passive)	• Responses with movement that is less or equally dynamic/animated than *talking*.
		• Responses with movement which should be static (i.e., a person lying down).
		• Responses in which the movement is reported as a picture, painting, caricature, or abstract piece of art, even with active movement reported in the art (i.e., a man running as a piece of artwork).
	a-p (active-passive)	• Responses in which two or more objects are described with movement and one is active and the other is passive (i.e., one dog biting another dog).

Note. Adapted description from *The Rorschach: A Comprehensive System.* Volume 1: *Basic Foundations,* 3rd ed. (pp. 109–113), by J. E. Exner, Jr., 1993, New York: John Wiley & Sons, Inc. Copyright 1993 by John Exner, Jr. Reprinted with permission.

- The coding goal is to determine how well or accurately an examinee's percept or response relates to the inkblot form, using Exner's Table A (explained below) as a guide.
- Coding a response ordinary (o) versus superior-overelaborated (+) can involve the examiner's subjective judgment.

How to Code Form Quality

- Use the transcribed text of the test and the location sheet to determine level of form quality. (Use only those responses that include some aspect of form.) Rapid Reference 3.8 summarizes form quality coding.

- Based on the location for each card, look up the form quality (FQ) description or category in Table A starting on page 195 of volume 1 or on page 101 of the Workbook (Exner, 1993; Exner, 1995). Table A provides a listing of responses, by card and location area for form quality codes ordinary (o), unusual (u), or minus (–). Table B starting on page 255 of volume 1 and on page 162 of the workbook provides illustrations of responses that should be coded superior-overelaborated (+) (Exner, 1993; Exner, 1995). Caret marks (<v>) are references to when the examinee turns the card to the left, upside down, or to the right to give a response.

≡ Rapid Reference 3.8

Form Quality Coding

For multiple objects,

1. Choose the most "conservative score" or lowest FQ level. A (– is lower than u and u is lower than o.)

2. The object with the lowest score should be important to the response.

If the response is formless (no form), do not code form quality.

- Table 3.5 provides a general description of Form Quality, but Table A is the primary source for empirically derived Form Quality scores (Exner, 1993).

- If the answer is not listed in Table A and is not a superior-elaborated response:

  1. Try to extrapolate conservatively from the answers in Table A. (For example, a top and a gyroscope are similar to each other and could be given the same form quality score.)

  2. If the object only has a remote similarity to an object in Table A, carefully consider the criteria between unusual and minus.

  3. Many responses contain multiple objects. Choose the lowest or most conservative score (minus, then unusual, then ordinary, then superior-elaborated), unless the object with the lowest form quality score is unimportant to the overall response. (For example, "Two dogs are looking at the same thing, maybe they are looking at a bug." The bug is less important than the two dogs doing the observing.)

Table 3.5   Form Quality

Symbol	Symbol Name	Explanation
+	Superior-overelaborated	• A response that is exceptionally precise and articulate and doesn't sacrifice the correct fit of the form. Response is unique in how the details are described and in how the form is used, however it is not necessarily an original answer. • May be listed in Table A as *o*, but response is usually well articulated, as in Table B. May not be listed in Table A or B.
o	Ordinary	• The obvious, commonplace, easily seen, and easily explained response that identifies an object frequently reported by others. • May not be listed in Table A as *o*.
u	Unusual	• An uncommon response, in which the contours of the inkblot are not significantly violated and the examiner can quickly and easily identify the object. • May not be listed in Table A as *u*.
–	Minus	• A distorted and unrealistic use of a form, in which the examiner can only identify the object with difficulty, or not at all. The response is imposed on the inkblot and disregards the structure of the inkblot. • May not be listed in Table A as –.

Note. Modified table from *The Rorschach: A Comprehensive System.* Volume 1: *Basic Foundations,* 3rd ed. (p. 152), by J. E. Exner, Jr., 1993, New York: John Wiley & Sons, Inc. Copyright 1993 by John Exner, Jr. Reprinted with permission.

4) Contents

- Contents refers to the name or class of object(s) used in the response, with 27 possible codes from whole human to x-ray (see Table 3.6).
- The coding goal is to categorize the objects described in the inkblot.

Table 3.6   Contents

Symbol	Symbol Name	Explanation (the response can include)
H	Whole Human	• A whole human figure.
		• If it is a *real* historical figure such as Joan of Arc, add secondary content code *Ay* (see below).
(H)	Whole Human (fictional or mythological)	• A whole fictional or mythological human figure, (i.e., a clown, fairy, giant, witch, fairytale creature, ghost, angel, science-fiction creature that is humanoid, humanlike monster.)
Hd	Human Detail	• An incomplete human form (i.e., a leg) or a whole form without a body part (i.e., a person without a head).
(Hd)	Human Detail (fictional or mythological)	• An incomplete fictional or mythological human figure (i.e., wings of an angel, arms of a witch).
		• All masks. (i.e., love, hate, sound, smell)
Hx	Human Experience	• Human emotional or sensory experience/ description (i.e., love, hate, sound, smell). Usually also scored special content *AB*.
A	Whole Animal	• A whole animal form.
(A)	Whole Animal (fictional or mythological)	• A whole fictional or mythological animal form (i.e., dragon, unicorn, Disney character).
Ad	Animal Detail	• An incomplete animal form (i.e., cat's head, claw of a crab, animal skin, rug made of animal skin).
(Ad)	Animal Detail (fictional or mythological)	• An incomplete fictional or mythological animal form (i.e., wings of Pegasus, parts of the body of a Disney character).
An	Anatomy	• Skeletal, muscular, organs or other internal anatomy without reference to x-ray (i.e., bones, skull, heart, vertebrae).

Table 3.6 continued

Symbol	Symbol Name	Explanation (the response can include)
		• If the response involves a laboratory tissue slide, add a secondary content code, *Art*.
		• If the response involves an X-ray, code only *Xy*.
Art	Art	• Paintings, drawings, illustrations, ranging in style from abstract to realism.
		• Art objects (i.e., statue, jewelry, chandelier, crest, seal, decoration).
		• Secondary content code for a laboratory tissue slide.
		• Many responses also have secondary content codes (i.e., a painting of two bears would be *Art, A*).
Ay	Anthropology	• Objects with a specific cultural and/or historical connotation even if still in use today (i.e., Arrowhead, prehistoric ax, Jewish menorah, Napolean's hat).
Bl	Blood	• Blood, either human or animal.
Bt	Botany	• Any type of plant life, individual parts or whole.
Cg	Clothing	• Any article of clothing.
Cl	Clouds	• Clouds. Used specifically as a reference to clouds. Any cloud variations (i.e., fog or mist) are coded *Na*.
Ex	Explosion	• A blast or explosion, including fireworks.
Fi	Fire	• Fire or smoke.
Fd	Food	• Anything edible.
Ge	Geography	• Any map, general or specific.

Table 3.6   continued

Symbol	Symbol Name	Explanation (the response can include)
Hh	Household	• Any household item used, inside or outside the house (except a lightbulb, which is coded *Sc*). • Rugs, except those made of animal skin, which are coded *Ad*.
Ls	Landscape	• Any form of landscape (i.e., mountains, underwater, deserts, swamps).
Na	Nature	• Anything from a natural environment that is not coded as *Bt* or *Ls*. • Anything astronomical or weather related (i.e., sun, planets, water, rainbow, fog, mist).
Sc	Science	• Anything associated with or that is a product of science or science fiction (i.e., computers, microscope, vehicle of transportation, rocket, lightbulb).
Sx	Sex	• Anything involving sex organs, activity of a sexual nature, or sexual reproduction (i.e., buttocks, menstruation, intercourse, abortion, breast—unless used to point out female figure). • *Sx* is usually scored as a secondary content. Primary contents are typically *H, Hd, An*.
Xy	X-Ray	• Any X-ray, skeletal or organs. When *Xy* is coded, *An* is not included as a secondary code.

Note. Modified table from *The Rorschach: A Comprehensive System.* Volume 1: *Basic Foundations,* 3rd ed. (pp. 158–59), by J. E. Exner, Jr., 1993, New York: John Wiley & Sons, Inc. Copyright 1993 by John Exner, Jr. Reprinted with permission.

How to Code Contents

- Use the transcribed text of the test to determine content.
- Many responses require more than one content code; however, each code can only be used once for a given response. Include all content codes with two exceptions:

  1. When a response includes *Na, Bt,* and/or *Ls,* only *Na* is scored.
  2. When a response includes both *Bt* and *Ls* (and *Na* is not present), score only one.

- Unique content that does not fit under any other content category receives an idiographic code (*Idio* or *Id*).

Rapid Reference 3.9 summarizes content coding rules.

5) Popular Responses

- Popular responses refers to frequently given responses.
- The coding goal is to determine whether the examinee's response is the conventional or commonly given response for each card.

How to Code Popular Responses

- Use the transcribed text of the test and location sheet to determine if the examinee's response is a popularly given response. For example, Card I's popular response is a bat or butterfly.
- Look up the examinee's description of the card in Table A, starting on page 195 in volume 1 or page 101 of the workbook (Exner, 1993; Exner, 1995). The first sentence below the card number provides the popular response(s) for that card. A more detailed description of the popular responses can be found in Table 24 on page 162 in volume 1 or Table 8 on page 57 of the workbook (Exner, 1993; Exner, 1995).
- Make sure the examinee's response uses the same location of the card as the popular response.
- Code a *P* if the answer is exactly the same as the popular response for that card. If it is not a popular response, no code is necessary and you can leave it blank.

6) Organizational Activity

- Organizational activity refers to the degree of organization required to integrate the form described in the response. It uses a Z score, a weighted method of assigning a score to a response.
- The coding goal is to provide a numerical Z score representing the degree of organizational activity.
- Every card has an organizational activity or Z score if the response includes form and meets at least one of the following criteria:

Rapid Reference 3.9

Content Rules

- A unique content response should be written out and entered under idiographic contents (Idio), in the Contents column.
- No duplicate codes for a given response.
- Responses can receive more than one content code with two exceptions:
  1. Only nature (Na) is scored even if a response includes nature (Na), botany (Bt) and/or landscape (Ls).
  2. For botany (Bt) and landscape (Ls) when nature (Na) is not present, score only one.

1. The location score is "whole" with developmental quality codes, either synthesized ($W+$), ordinary (Wo), or vague synthesized ($Wv/+$).
2. It meaningfully integrates at least two adjacent or nonadjacent parts of the inkblot (portions that may or may not touch).
3. It meaningfully integrates white space.

Rapid Reference 3.10 summarizes when not to code a Z score.

How to Code Organizational Activity

- Use the location codes and the developmental quality (DQ) codes, scored earlier, to determine the Z score.
- Determine if the card meets criteria (see Rapid Reference 3.11) for a Z value and which category the response could fit (ZW, Zadj, Zdis, ZS).
- Look up the organizational (Z) values based on the type of organizational activity for each of the 10 cards in one of the following sources:

Rapid Reference 3.10

Don't Code for a Z Score

Responses never receive an organizational score if:

1. Dv.
2. white space or without reference to the white space.
3. no form involvement (i.e., pure C, T, Y, or V).
4. Special Score, CONFAB.

1. The table called Organizational (Z) Values on the Notes and Calculations page of the Structural Summary Blank
2. Table 20 on page 147 of volume 1 (Exner, 1993)
3. Table 8 on page 60 of the Workbook (Exner, 1995)

• If the response meets more than one category's criteria, choose the category with the highest Z value for that card.

• Remember that form must always be involved to receive a Z score, so pure *C, T, Y,* or *V* responses are never coded with an organizational activity score.

7) Special Scores

• Special scores refers to the presence of an unusual characteristic(s) in the response, with 16 possible scores from deviant verbalizations to color projection (see Table 3.7).

• The coding goal is to categorize the unusual verbalizations.

CAUTION 3.2

Demographic Variables and Level 1 and Level 2 Scores

Demographic variables such as age, education, or culture are not considered in distinguishing level 1 and level 2 scores. These elements are considered during the interpretation stage when comparing an examinee's scores with the scores listed in the descriptive statistics tables.

How to Code Special Scores

• Use the transcribed text of the test to determine special scores.
• For deviant verbalizations (*DV, DR*) and inappropriate combinations (*INCOM* and *FABCOM*), determine the degree of cognitive slippage or bizarreness, represented as level 1 and level 2 responses (see Table 3.8) Caution box 3.2 warns exam-

≡ Rapid Reference 3.11

When to Code for a Z Score

- The examiner should code for a Z score if a response includes form and meets at least one of the following criteria:
  1. ZW: It has a location code W and a Developmental Quality code of +, v/+, or o (answers with a Wv are not assigned a score).
  2. ZAdj: It is a response that meaningfully integrates separate objects in adjacent areas of the inkblot (areas that touch).
  3. ZDis: It is a response that meaningfully integrates separate objects in nonadjacent areas of the inkblot (areas that don't touch).
  4. ZS: It is a response that meaningfully integrates white space with other details of the inkblot in the description (such as "eyes in a face").
- If a response meets criteria for more than one category, choose the score with the highest Z value for that card.

Note. Adapted descriptions from Exner (1993), p. 16.

iners not to consider an examiner's demographic information when coding level 1 and 2 scores.

- It is not uncommon for a response to receive more than one special score; however, exceptions and certain exclusionary rules are listed in Rapid Reference 3.12. Use these rules to avoid inflating the total sum of special scores.
- The same wording or the same instance of cognitive confusion never receives more than one special score. Verbiage much be completely independent to receive more than one special score.

Caution 3.3 summarizes what examiners should keep in mind when coding an examinee's responses.

CAUTION 3.3

The Coding Process

- The examiner should take his or her time coding. With inaccurate coding, the examiner unintentionally creates the foundation for an inaccurate interpretation.
- Scan each response carefully and review options. Be aware of errors of omission and over coding.
- Reliability studies suggest greater disparity between examiners by omissions than by coding disagreements (Exner, 1993).

Table 3.7 Special Scores

Category	Symbol Name	Level	Explanation
Unusual Verbalizations	(DV) Deviant Verbalizations	Neologism	• An incorrect word or neologism in place of a correct one when the examinee has the verbal capacity.
			✦ DV1: Some bacteria you might see under a *telescope* (instead of *microscope*).
			• DV2: A woman is ready for a *virginal* exam.
		Redundancy	• Odd language repeating information about the object(s) reported. The response can not be justified by subcultural idioms or limited vocabulary.
			✦ DV1: a *pair* of *two* birds. DV2: a *backward reversed* propeller of an airplane.
	(DR) Deviant Responses	Inappropriate Phrases	• Phrases that are inappropriate or completely irrelevant.
			✦ DR1: It's a cat. *My father always hated cats.*
			• DR2: An abstract of President Carter *if you look at it from a Democratic perspective.*
		Circumstantial Responses	• Fluid or rambling answers in which the examinee inappropriately elaborates or has marked difficulty in achieving a definition of the object. Sometimes wandering off target and never returning to subject.

Table 3.7   continued

Category	Symbol Name	Level	Explanation
			♦ DR2: *I'm a mechanic,* so I can tell it's a car, *but I'm not sure how to look at it. I can see the back wheel and brake, which should always be checked* . . .
Inappropriate Combination	(INCOM) Incongruous Combination		• Inappropriately merging separate inkblot details or images into a single object. Coded *only* when the combination describes a single object.
			♦ INCOM1: An orange man. INCOM2: A woman with the head of a chicken.
	(FABCOM) Fabulized Combination		• An implausible or unbelievable relationship is described between two or more objects in the inkblot.
			♦ FABCOM1: Two chickens *holding basketballs.* FABCOM2: A man sitting there *and you can see his heart pumping.*
	(CONTAM) Contamination		• The most bizarre of the inappropriate combinations. Two or more impressions fused into a single response in a manner that clearly violates reality. The objects might otherwise be reported separately.
			• Involves a single discrete area of the inkblot.
			♦ CONTAM: It must be a *bird dog* because it has the body of a dog and the nose of a bird.

Table 3.7   continued

Category	Symbol Name	Level	Explanation
(ALOG) Inappropriate Logic			• Without prompting, spontaneously uses strained, unconventional, or loose logic to justify a response.
			• ALOG: It's white *so it must be from an angel.*
Perseveration and Integration Failure	(PSV) Perseveration	Within Card Perseveration	• Within one card, consecutive answers that have exactly the same location, determinant, content, DQ, FQ, and Z scores. Content score can change as long as it stays within the same category. Popular and Special scores need not be the same.
			• Examinee gives two separate answers, not an alternative answer to card.
			• *PSV* on Card I: This could be a bat or it could be a butterfly, too.
		Content Perseveration	• Answer that identifies an object that was seen previously. Object can be engaged in a different activity.
			• *PSV* on Card I and Card V: Oh, there's that butterfly again, this time it's sitting on a branch.
		Mechanical Perseveration	• Mechanistic report of the same object over and over again, usually by examinees who are cognitively and/or neurologically impaired.
			• *PSV* on Cards I, II, III, etc.: It's a bat.

Table 3.7   continued

Category	Symbol Name	Level	Explanation
	(CONFAB) Confabulation		• Inappropriate generalization from one detailed area to the whole inkblot. • Z score and ALOG are not coded. ♦ CONFAB: It's a claw, it's a lobster.
Special Content Characteristics	(AG) Aggressive Movement		• Movement response with current aggression (no past tense).
	(COP) Cooperative Movement		• Movement response with a clearly positive or cooperative interaction.
	(MOR) Morbid Content		• An object is identified as dead, destroyed, ruined, spoiled, damaged, injured, or broken. • An object is attributed as having a clearly dysphoric feeling or characteristic such as a sad tree.
Other Special Features	(AB) Abstract Content		• Human Experience (Hx) content coded answers noting human emotion or sensory experience. • Clear and specific symbolic representation of an object when form is used. An abstract painting is scored only when specific representation is noted, such as it represents the struggle for power.

Table 3.7 continued

Category	Symbol Name	Level	Explanation
	(PER) Personalized Answers		• Refers to personal knowledge or experience as part of the basis for justifying and /or clarifying a response.
			• Response needs to include more than just general commentary or a reference to self (i.e., not just "*I* think it looks like . . ." but, "My mother showed me . . .")
	(CP) Color Projection		• Identifies an achromatic (black-white) area of the inkblot as chromatic (colors of the rainbow).

Note. Adapted from Exner (1993), pp. 166–74.

Rapid Reference 3.12

Exclusionary Rules for Special Scores

1. If *CONFAB*, never include *ALOG*, even if *ALOG* is in the response.
2. If *CONTAM*, never include *DV, DR, INCOM, FABCOM,* or *ALOG*, even if in the response.
3. If *DV, DR, INCOM, FABCOM,* or *ALOG*:
   a. The verbiage meeting criterion for each of these scores must be completely separate from the others.
   b. When criteria overlap, code only one special score and use a step-up rule: pick the score with the highest weighted value from *Wsum6*. [Weighted values: *ALOG* (5), *FABCOM* (4, 7), *DR* (3, 6), *INCOM* (2, 4), *DV* (1, 2)].

Table 3.8   Special Scores Level 1 and Level 2

Level 1 Responses	• Mild or modest instances of illogical, fluid, particular, or circumstantial thinking. Responses are similar to cognitive slips that occur when people are not paying close attention to how they are expressing themselves or to the judgments they are making.
	• Responses sound like products of immaturity, lack of education, judgments that are not well thought out, or careless errors.
Level 2 Responses	• Moderate or severe dissociated, illogical, fluid, or circumstantial thinking. Expressing flawed judgment and/or a very unusual mode of talking.
	• Responses stand out because of their bizarreness and seldom create scoring doubts. When the examiner has legitimate doubts about whether a response meets level 2 criteria, take a conservative stance and assign a level 1 score.

Note. Adapted descriptions from Exner (1993), p. 166.

TRANSFERRING CODES TO THE SEQUENCE OF SCORES SHEET

The Sequence of Scores sheet has 10 columns listing all the coding scores for each response. One of Exner's computer-generated Sequence of Scores sheet is shown in Table 3.9. If hand-scoring, it might be best for the new examiner to fill out the Sequence of Scores sheet after completing the coding using our Scoring worksheet in order to insure greater accuracy, while the more advanced examiner might fill out the Sequence of Scores sheet at the same time as he or she codes the responses.

If computer scoring, some examiners use computer software such as RIAP or ROR-SCAN interpretive reports, specifically designed for the Exner Comprehensive System. In these cases, the examiner codes the re-

Table 3.9 Scoring Sequence for Protocol L.S.

Card	No	Loc	#	Determinant(s)	(2)	Content(s)	POP	Z	Special Scores
I	1	Wo	1	FMpo		A	P	1.0	
	2	W+	1	Ma-po	2	H, (A)		4.0	AB, COP
	3	Ddo	24	Fo		Sc			
II	4	D+	6	FMpo	2	Ad	P	3.0	
	5	DS+	5	ma.CFo		Sc, Fi		4.5	
III	6	D+	1	Ma+	2	H, Ls	P	3.0	COP
	7	Do	3	FCo		Cg			
IV	8	W+	1	FMp.FD.FTo		A, Bt		4.0	
	9	Do	3	FYo		Bt			PER
V	10	Wo	1	Fo		A	P	1.0	DR
VI	11	Wo	1	FTo		Ad	P	2.5	
	12	Do	4	ma.FYo		Sc			
	13	Do	3	Fo		Ay			
VII	14	D+	1	Fo	2	Hd, Id	P	1.0	
	15	Do	2	Fo		A			
	16	W+	1	Ma+	2	H		3.0	COP
VIII	17	Wo	1	CFo	2	Art		4.5	
	18	Do	1	Fo		A	P		
	19	Do	4	FMa.FDu		A			
IX	20	Do	4	Fo		Hd			
	21	Do	8	Fo		Hh			
	22	D+	1	Ma.mpo		H, Sc		2.5	
X	23	Do	1	Fo	2	A	P		
	24	Do	7	FMao		A			
	25	W+	1	CFo	2	Bt		5.5	

Note. Copyright © 1976, 1985, 1990 by John E. Exner, Jr.

sponses and then enters the scores into the computer program. While examiners use these software packages because they generate both the Structural Summary and interpretative information (discussed in the next several chapters), the printout of the Sequence of Scores sheet that comes with it is an added advantage.

In Conjunction with our Scoring worksheet

If the examiner has used our Scoring worksheet, filling in the Sequence of Scores sheet will take only a few minutes. At the end of the coding process, the examiner should have one Scoring worksheet for each response. The codes from these pages are now transferred to the Sequence of Scores sheet. Note that the worksheet's sections match the Sequence of Scores columns. Use Table 3.10 for directions and helpful tips on how to transfer the codes and make the notations.

Without our Scoring Worksheet

The examiner can choose to fill in the Sequence of Scores sheet during the coding process. The examiner may want to use a pencil rather than a pen, so corrections look neater. Use Table 3.10 for directions and helpful tips for filling in what codes goes in each column of the Sequence of Scores sheet.

Table 3.10 Filling in the Sequence of Scores Sheet

Column Name	What Codes Go in the Column?	General Tips
Card	Card number	• Use Roman numerals.
Resp. No.	Response number	• Use Arabic numerals and number continuously. Do not renumber each card.
Location and DQ	Location codes (W, D, Dd, S) and Developmental Quality codes (+, v/+, o, v)	• List Location code(s) first. *S* is listed after *W, D,* or *Dd.* • After Location codes, list Developmental Quality code.
Loc. No.	Location number code	• List number. If DQ is a *W* may be leave blank or insert a dash (-).

Table 3.10 continued

Column Name	What Codes Go in the Column?	General Tips
Determinant(s) and Form Quality	Determinants with form quality determinants	• List determinants, which are separated by a full stop (.) or periods. Movement is listed first, followed by form, color, and shading (in no particular order). Reflections are listed last under blends. (Some instructors prefer to list determinants based on the order they appear in the response.) • Active and passive superscripts immediately follow a movement determinant. • At the end of the row, the last code should be form quality (if the response has form).
(2)	Pairs determinants (2)	• List as (2), if scored.
Content(s)	Contents	• List one after another in the order they were stated.
Pop	Popular Responses	• List *P,* if scored.
Z Score	Organizational Activity	• List numeric Z score.
Special Scores	Special Scores	• List one after another in the order they were stated. • For *DV, INC, DR, FAB,* after the special score code note if level 1 or 2.

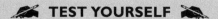 **TEST YOURSELF**

1. **What is the cardinal rule of coding?**
2. **What is the best resource for coding rules?**
   (a) this Essentials book
   (b) Exner's Volume 1
   (c) Exner's Workbook
   (d) all of the above
   (e) b and c
3. **Specific form demand does not necessarily mean it has a specific shape.** True or False?
4. **Almost all responses have a form, so a first-time examiner knows that he or she can almost always code an F.** True or False?
5. **If the examinee's content can't be listed under any of the other categories, do not use idiographic (*Id* or *Idio*) unless the examiner has sent a letter to the Rorschach Workshops informing them of the unusual response.** True or False?

Answers: 1. The code or score should represent the cognitive operation at the time the examinee gave the answer; 2. b; 3. False; 4. False; 5. False.

Four

HOW TO CREATE A STRUCTURAL SUMMARY FOR THE RORSCHACH

Tara Rose

UPPER AND LOWER SECTIONS OF THE STRUCTURAL SUMMARY

The Structural Summary compiles all of one examinee's scores. It includes two sections, upper and lower. The upper section records the frequency with which each variable appeared in the record, while the lower section records ratios, percentages, and derived scores, as well as special indices. For examiners using a computer program such as the RIAP that prints out the upper and lower half of the Structural Summary, this chapter demonstrates the long-hand process of how the final scores are generated.

The upper section of the Structural Summary form is completed first and is primarily based on information from the Sequence of Scores sheet. The lower section is completed second and is primarily based on the frequencies tallied from the upper section and the results from the Constellations Worksheet, with a few frequencies from the Sequence of Scores sheet. This chapter will cover in detail how to score each section. The instructions rely on the template and numbering system we created to help examiners quickly and accurately hand-score the lower half of the Structural Summary form for template (see Appendixes 5a and 5b).

The template is very easy to use. The directions for preparing the template —essentially photocopying the pages in Appendix 5a and 5b onto clear sheets or transparencies—are explained in Rapid Reference 4.1. The template is placed on top of the upper half of the Structural Summary form and is aligned with the variables so that each variable has its own number. (For example, a $\boxed{1}$ will appear to the left of the variable Zf and a $\boxed{2}$ will appear to the left of the variable Zsum.) With this template and numbering system, the first-time examiner will save at least an hour scoring his or her first Rorschach, including

≡ *Rapid Reference 4.1*

Preparing the Transparency Template

1. Photocopy the templates from Appendixes 5a and 5b onto an 8" x 11" transparency. Do not enlarge or reduce the size of the form. (It's often easiest to take the book to a full-service photocopy store where you can purchase a single transparency and have them photocopy it for you.)

2. Place the photocopied transparency on top of the Structural Summary form.

3. Use the L-shaped indices at the corners of the transparency to align it with the Structural Summary form. Make sure the boxed numbers on the transparency are located to the left of the variables underneath.

4. Secure the transparency to the form using a binder or paper clip on one corner. Once the transparency is secure, the examiner can flip the transparency up and down without needing to realign the transparency to the form each time.

5. The examiner may want to make a second photocopy of the transparency clipped to the Structural Summary form on plain paper so that there is a permanent record of the variables and their corresponding numbers.

the time it takes to prepare the template. If you are unable to photocopy the template, use the numbering system and hand-print the numbers to the left of each score on the upper half of the Structural Summary form. This process will take only a few minutes.

STEP BY STEP: THE UPPER SECTION (U)

The first step in the scoring process is to obtain the frequencies or counts of each variable. Almost all of the information needed to create these scores is located on the Sequence of Scores sheet. Much of the scoring in the upper portion of the form is fairly straightforward. Difficulty arises either in locating the necessary information or feeling certain that the calculated numbers are correct. With these step-by-step directions, the examiner will be able to both quickly locate the information and feel confident about how the scores were obtained.

The upper section is comprised of seven areas: Location Features; Determinants; Form Quality; Contents; Organizational Activity; Populars, Pairs, and Reflections; and Special Scores. The directions for each of these steps will rely on the transparency template and the numbering system associated with the template, so *the examiner should make the transparency before continuing.*

Again, if you are pressed for time or are not able to make the transparency, hand-print the numbers on the upper half of the Structural Summary form to correspond with our scoring system.

Now you are ready to begin scoring. For each section you will find a table providing scoring directions. As you fill in the upper portion of the Structural Summary form, leave the area for the variable blank if there are no scores to tally. There are two exceptions to this rule explained in Caution 4.1.

LOCATION FEATURES: SCORES $\boxed{1}$ – $\boxed{16}$ (U.1)

There are three areas under Location Features: Organizational Activity, Location Codes, and Developmental Quality.

Organizational Activity: Scores $\boxed{1}$ – $\boxed{3}$ (U.1.1)

To begin, for Zf or the Z frequency score, look under the Z-Score column on the Sequence of Scores sheet. Count the number of times there is a Z-score for a response. For Zsum, refer to the same Z-score column, tally the Z-score numbers for all responses. For Zest, take the Zf score and look it up on the Zest table from the Notes and Calculations sheet of the Structural Summary Blank. You can also find the Zest in Table 27 on page 182 of Vol. 1 and in Table 10 on page 87 of the Workbook (Exner, 1993; Exner, 1995). For quick directions on scoring organizational activity, see Table 4.1.

Location Codes: Scores $\boxed{4}$ – $\boxed{8}$ (U.1.2)

For the location code score, look under the Location and DQ column on the Sequence of Scores sheet and count the total number

---

> ### CAUTION 4.1
>
> #### Filling in blank scores
>
> On the upper portion of the form: Leave the area for the variable blank if there are no scores to tally.
> There are two exceptions to this rule:
>
> (1) For Form Quality (FQ–) scores ($\boxed{13}$ – $\boxed{16}$), zeros should be filled in when appropriate.
>
> (2) For Contents, if a content has only a secondary score, a zero and a comma should be placed before the tally of the secondary score (i.e., 0, #).

Table 4.1 Organizational Activity

Variable Name	Variable Number	Directions for Scoring
Zf	$\boxed{1}$	Look under the Z-Score column for Z-Scores. Count the total number of Z-Scores.
Zsum	$\boxed{2}$	Look under the Z-Score column. Add up all the scores for a total sum.
Zest	$\boxed{3}$	Using the "Best Weighted Zsum Prediction When Zf Is Known" table on the Notes and Calculations sheet (or in Vol. 1 or the Workbook), look up the Z-score or $\boxed{1}$ to find the Zest. (The Zest score is to the right of the Zf score.)

Table 4.2 Location Codes

Variable Name	Variable Number	Directions for Scoring
W	$\boxed{4}$	Count the total number of W's in the Location and DQ column. (Include Wv's.)
Wv	$\boxed{5}$	Same as $\boxed{4}$, but count the total number of Wv's (Do not include W's.)
D	$\boxed{6}$	Same as $\boxed{4}$, but count the total number of D's. (Do not include Dd's.)
Dd	$\boxed{7}$	Same as $\boxed{4}$, but count the total number of Dd's.
S	$\boxed{8}$	Same as $\boxed{4}$, but count the total number of S's.

of occurences of each location code (W, Wv, D, Dd, S). See Table 4.2 for directions on scoring location codes.

Hint: When counting W's, D's, and Dd's, don't worry about the S's in the same row.

DQ—Developmental Quality: Scores $\boxed{9}$ – $\boxed{16}$ (U.1.3)

For the first five variables, focus solely on the Developmental Quality (DQ) of the responses. Do not focus on the actual location of the responses. Look under the Location and DQ column on the Sequence of Scores sheet and count the total number of occurrences of each Developmental Quality.

Table 4.3   Developmental Quality (DQ)

Variable Name	Variable Number	Directions for Scoring
+	9	Count the total number of +'s in the Location and DQ column.
o	10	Same as 9, but count the total number of *o*'s.
v/+	11	Same as 9, but count the total number of *v*/+'s.
v	12	Same as 9, but count the total number of *v*'s.

Table 4.4   Developmental Quality (DQ) and Form Quality Minus (FQ–)

Variable Name	Variable Number	Directions for Scoring
+(FQ–)	13	Go back and look at the rows with pluses in the Location and DQ column, then search for minuses at the end of the row in the Determinants and Form Quality column. Count how many times this occurs.
o(FQ–)	14	Same as 13, but first look for *o*'s. Then look for the minuses at the end of the row. Count the number of times this occurs.
v/+(FQ–)	15	Same as 13, but first look for *v*/+'s. Then look for the minuses at the end of the row. Count the number of times this occurs.
v(FQ–)	16	Same as 13, but first look for *v*'s. Then look for the minuses at the end of the row. Count the number of times this occurs.

The next four variable scores do take into consideration both the Developmental Quality (DQ) and the Form Quality Minus (*FQ*–). First, for each Developmental Quality score (+, *o*, *v*/+, *v*), look in the Location and DQ column of the Sequence of Scores sheet and locate the occurrences (as done for scores 9 through 12). Second, search the Determinants and Form Quality column for a Form Quality Minus code ("–") at the end of the row. Count how many minus signs there are for each Developmental Quality score and write this score within the parentheses provided to the right of the Developmental Quality codes on the Structural Summary form. See Tables 4.3 and 4.4 for Developmental Quality.

DETERMINANTS: SCORES 17 – 41 (U.2)

There are three sections to complete under Determinants. The first is a list of blends in which multiple determinant responses are written out, one response beneath another. The second section is a column of all possible single determinants. The third section has only one variable, pairs, and is located just below the column of single determinants.

Blends: Score 17 (U.2.1)

Blends are short lists of the multiple response determinants and listed under score 17. A multiple response is identified by at least one period between codes under the Determinants and Form Quality column on the Sequence of Scores sheet (e.g., *Cn.Fr*). The determinants are rewritten under the heading Blends on the Structural Summary form, one response below the next, forming a column, in the order that they were recorded. Only the determinants are rewritten, do not attach active-passive superscripts or Form Qualities (+, *o*, *u*, or –). Do, however, include the periods between each determinant. For example, *FM^p.FD.FT*+ becomes *FM.FD.FT,* while *M^{ap}.mp* becomes *M.m,* and *m^{a}CF*– becomes *m.CF.*

Singles: Scores 18 – 40 (U.2.2)

Singles comprise scores 18 through 40 and refer to all of the singular determinants under the Determinant and Form Quality column. Singular determinants are responses in which only one determinant has been coded for a single response (and should not have been listed under Blends). To tally single determinants, look under the Determinant and Form Quality column and

Table 4.5   Single Determinants

Variable name	Variable Number	Variable name	Variable Number
M	18	T	30
FM	19	FV	31
m	20	VF	32
FC	21	V	33
CF	22	FY	34
C	23	YF	35
Cn	24	Y	36
FC'	25	Fr	37
C'F	26	Rf	38
C'	27	FD	39
FT	28	F	40
TF	29		

Note: Here are directions for Scoring *M* through *F*. Look under the Determinants and Form Quality column on the Sequence of Scores sheet. Count the total number of times each single determinant occurs. Do not include determinants from Blends.

note the responses that have only one determinant coded. Count the total number of each of the 27 single determinants. Complete this process for each determinant, scores 18 through 40. (See Table 4.5 for single determinants and their corresponding numbers.)

Pairs or (2): Score 41 (U.2.3)

Pairs or (2), score 41, refers to the pair response determinant. Pairs or (2) has its own small area below the Single Determinants column on the Structural Summary form, labeled (2). For this score, count the total number of *2*'s in the (2) column of the Sequence of Scores sheet and write the number on the Structural Summary form.

Table 4.6   Form Quality Extended (FQx)

Variable Name	Variable Number	Directions for Scoring
FQx +	42	Look under the Determinants and Form Quality column for a + at the end of the row. Count the number of times this occurs.
FQx o	43	Same as 42, but look for an o at the end of the row. Count the number of times this occurs.
FQx u	44	Same as 42, but look for a u at the end of the row. Count the number of times this occurs.
FQx –	45	Same as 42, but look for a minus, at the end of the row. Count the number of times this occurs.
FQ none (where no Form Quality has been listed)	46	Same as 42, but for the omission of Form Quality. If the entire response is formless (i.e., there is no form involvement, no +, o, u, – at the end of the row), then no Form Quality was coded. Count the number of times this occurs.

Form Quality: Scores 42 – 60 (U.3)

There are four categories of formulas under Form Quality: Fqx, Fqf, Mqual, and Sqx.

FQx — Form Quality Extended: Scores 42 – 46 (U.3.1)

FQx means Form Quality Extended and reflects a count of all Form Qualities (+, *o, u,* –) in the recorded responses (see Table 4.6). All responses that include a form are coded for Form Quality so the information in this section will appear under the Determinants and Form Quality column on the Sequence of Scores sheet. For these scores, count the number of occurrences for each Form Quality (+, *o, u,* –), as well as when there is no occurrence of Form Quality. Enter the number under scores 42 – 46.

Table 4.7   Form Quality–Form (FQf)

Variable Name	Variable Number	Directions for Scoring
F+	47	First, look under the Determinants and Form Quality column for *only* pure *F*'s (no other determinants). Second, search for a + at the end of the row in that same column. Count the number of times this occurs.
Fo	48	Same as 47, but look for an *o* at the end of the row. Count the number of times this occurs.
Fu	49	Same as 47, but look for a *u* at the end of the row. Count the number of times this occurs.
F–	50	Same as 47, but look for a – at the end of the row. Count the number of times this occurs.

Hint: If the entire response is formless, then no Form Quality is coded.

FQf — Form Quality – Form: Scores 47 – 50 *(U.3.2)*

FQf means Form Quality–Form and reflects the total number of Form Quality responses when pure form (*F*) is recorded (see Table 4.7). To tally, first count the number of *F* only determinants under the Determinants and Form Quality column. Remember, there should be no other determinants included on the response line (no *CF, FC, C'F, FC', TF, FT, VF, FV, YF, FY,* or *FD*). Second, go to the end of the row in the same Determinants and Form Quality column and count the total occurrences of each Form Quality code (+, *o, u,* –).

Mqual — Form Quality Human Movement: Scores 51 – 55 *(U.3.3)*

Mqual means Form Quality of Human Movement and reflects the total number of times there is a form quality when human movement (*M*) is recorded

Table 4.8   Form Quality of Only Human Movement (*Mqual*)

Variable Name	Variable Number	Directions for Scoring
M+	51	First, look under the Determinants and Form Quality column for all combinations that include *M*. Then look for the plus sign at the end of that row in that same column. Count the number of times this occurs.
Mo	52	Same as 51, but look for an *o* at the end of the row. Count the number of times this occurs.
Mu	53	Same as 51, but look for a *u* at the end of the row. Count the number of times this occurs.
M–	54	Same as 51, but look for a – at the end of the row. Count the number of times this occurs.
M none	55	Same as 51, but look for an omission of form quality. The entire response should be formless (i.e., there is no form involvement, no +, *o*, *u*, – at the end of the row). Count the number of times this occurs.

(see Table 4.8). To tally, first look under the Determinants and Form Quality column and find all *M* determinants. Second, for those responses with *M*, go to the end of the row in the same Determinants and Form Quality column and count the total occurrences of each form quality (+, *o*, *u*, –).

SQx — Form Quality – Space: Scores 56 – 60 *(U.3.4)*

SQx means Form Quality–Space and reflects the form quality when white space is being used (see Table 4.9). To tally, first look under the Location and DQ column and find the recorded responses that include space determinants (*S*'s). Second, for those responses with space (*S*), go to the Determinants and Form Quality column and see if there is a +, *o*, *u*, or – at the end of that row. Count the total occurrences of each form quality (+, *o*, *u*, –).

Table 4.9   Form Quality–Space (SQx)

Variable Name	Variable Number	Directions for Scoring
S+	56	First, look in the Location and DQ column first for any combinations that include *S*. Then search the Determinants and Form Quality column for a + at the end of the row. Count the number of times this occurs.
So	57	Same as 56, but look for an *o* at the end of the row. Count the number of times this occurs.
Su	58	Same as 56, but look for a *u* at the end of the row. Count the number of times this occurs.
S–	59	Same as 56, but look for a – at the end of the row. Count the number of times this occurs.
S none	60	Same as 56, but look for an omission of form quality. The entire response should be formless (i.e., there is no form involvement, no +, *o*, *u*, or – at the end of the row). Count the number of times this occurs.

Contents: Scores 61 – 87 (U.4)

The section Contents on the Structural Summary form lists the total frequencies from the 27 content categories. To complete this section, look under the Content(s) column of the Sequence of Scores sheet. Note that sometimes the Content(s) column has only one content variable listed, while other times, multiple variables are listed with a period in between each score. When more than one variable listed, the first score is a primary content variable or score, while the second and subsequent scores are secondary content variables (see Rapid Reference 4.2). For each primary content score, count the number of single content variables along with the total number of primary content variables listed. For each secondary content score, count the total number of secondary content variables listed. Repeat for each content score, *H* to *Idio*, scores 61 to 87. (See Table 4.10).

The format for writing down the contents frequencies under the Contents column of the Structural Summary form is similar to format used in the Con-

Table 4.10   Contents

Variable Name	Variable Number	Variable Name	Variable Number
H	61	Cg	75
(H)	62	Cl	76
Hd	63	Ex	77
(Hd)	64	Fd	78
Hx	65	Fi	79
A	66	Ge	80
(A)	67	Hh	81
Ad	68	Ls	82
(Ad)	69	Na	83
An	70	Sc	84
Art	71	Sx	85
Ay	72	Xy	86
Bl	73	Idio	87
Bt	74		

Note: Here are directions for Scoring *H* through *Indio*. Look under the Contents column on the Sequence of Scores sheet and look for each variable. Count the number of times each variable occurs as a primary content and as a secondary content score. If there is a secondary content score, first list the primary content and then list the secondary content score. Separate the two scores with a comma.

tent(s) column of the Sequence of Scores sheet. When tallying scores, the primary content score total is listed first, followed by a comma, and the secondary content score is listed second (i.e., 2,1 or 0,2). A secondary content total score is listed only if a content category has a secondary content score in the Content(s) column on the Sequence of Scores sheet. In other words, if there is no secondary content, the comma and the zero are not necessary. (For example, a 1 is fine, the examiner does not need to write 1,0).

Approach Summary: Scores 88 – 97 (U.5)

The section titled Approach Summary appears on the top righthand corner of the Structural Summary form. Scoring is straightforward and requires the examiner to list the location approach for each card. The necessary scores can be found under the Location and DQ column on the Sequences of Scores sheet. List the location scores (*W, D, Dd, S*) that were used for each card, response by response, with a period between each response. For example, for Card I (score 88), the score could be *W* with one response, *W.D* with two responses, *W.D.DdS* with three responses, and so on. Note that some computer generated Structural Summaries have dropped this section and replaced it with the Suicide Potential Constellation Index discussed later in this chapter (L.8.1).

Special Scorings: Scores 98 through 117 (U. 6)

The Special Scorings section appears below the Approach Summary on the righthand side of the Structural Summary form. There are three short sections to complete. The first section is a tally of the first six special scores with a distinction made between level 1 and level 2 scores. The second section is an additive equation of all the scores in the first section, and the third section is a tally of the last eight special scores.

≡*Rapid Reference 4.2*

Primary Content Versus Secondary Content

The *Primary Content* represents the total number of single content scores (variables listed by themselves in the Content(s) column) *and* the total number of primary content scores (variables listed first and before the comma in the Content(s) column when two contents are listed).

The *Secondary Content* represents the total number of secondary content scores (those variables listed second and after the comma in the Content(s) column when two contents are listed).

DV, INC, DR, FAB: Scores 98 – 107 (U.6.1)

The first section of the special scores begins with counting the total number of *DV, INC, DR,* and *FAB* level 1 and level 2 scores that occurred in the record, followed by counting the *ALOG* and *CON* Special Scores (see Table 4.11).

Look under the Special Scores column on the Sequence of Scores sheet and tally each *DV, INC, DR,* and *FAB* level 1 and level 2 special score. If reviewing other examiners' Rorschach Blanks, please note that the distinction between level 1 and level 2 scores for *DV, INC, DR,* and *FAB* are not always written as clearly as they could be. Sometimes, when an examiner lists the scores, he or she notes the level only if it is a level 2 score and otherwise leaves out the level 1 notation (i.e., *FAB* meaning FAB, Level 1; and *FAB2* meaning FAB, Level 2). If the examiner has not listed the distinction between level 1 and level 2 scores on the Sequence of Scores sheet, he or she must either recall from memory or look back at the Rorschach Coding Worksheet to determine whether the response is a level 1 or level 2 score.

To total the number of *ALOG* and *CON* scores, look under the Special Scores column on the Sequence of Scores sheet and count the number of times each occurs. There is only one level for these scores.

Raw Sum 6 and Weighted Sum 6: Scores 108 *and* 109 *(U.6.2)*

In this section, tally the *Raw Sum6* (RSum6) and Weighted Sum6 (*Wgtd Sum6*) scores using the values from *DV, NC, DR, FAB, LOG,* and *CON* listed above (scores 98 – 107). Raw Sum6 is simply a sum score, while Weighted Sum6 score applies weights for each value in Raw Sum 6 (see Table 4.12).

AB, AG, CFB, COP, MOR, PER, PSV: Scores 110 *–* 117 *(U.6.3)*

The final portion of the upper section of the Structural Summary, Special Scores, takes only a few moments to complete. Tally the total counts of the final eight special scores (*AB, AG, CFB, COP, CP, MOR, PER,* and *PSV*), scores 110 – 117, which are located in the Special Scores column of the Sequence of Scores sheet (see Table 4.13).

STEP-BY-STEP: THE LOWER SECTION (L)

Completing the scores for the lower section is the final step to the Structural Summary. The scores in this section will later be used for interpreting the responses, which is discussed in the next chapter. The information needed to create these scores is located on the upper section of the Structural Summary form, the Sequence of Scores sheet, and the Constellations Worksheet.

The lower section has seven data blocks and one special indices section. The seven data blocks are Core, Ideation, Affect, Mediation, Processing, Interpersonal, and Self-perception (see Rapid Reference 4.3). Making up the special indices section are six special indices scores which go across the bottom of the page: *SCZI, DEPI, CDI, S-Con, HVI,* and *OBS* (see Rapid Reference 4.4). This

Table 4.11 Special Scores DV through CON

Variable Name	Variable Number	Directions for Scoring
DV	Lvl. 1 [98] Lvl. 2 [99]	Look at the Special Scores column of the Sequence of Scores sheet and look for *DV* responses. Count the total number of Lvl. 1 (Level 1) and Lvl. 2 (Level 2) scores.
INC	Lvl. 1 [100] Lvl. 2 [101]	Same as [98] and [99], but count the total number of *INC* Lvl. 1 and Lvl. 2 scores.
DR	Lvl. 1 [102] Lvl. 2 [103]	Same as [98] and [99], but count the total number of *DR* Lvl. 1 and Lvl. 2 scores.
FAB	Lvl. 1 [104] Lvl. 2 [105]	Same as [98] and [99], but count the total number of *FAB* Lvl. 1 and Lvl. 2 scores.
ALOG	[106]	Look under the Special Scores column on the Sequence of Scores sheet. Count the number of times *ALOG* occurs.
CON	[107]	Look under the Special Scores column on the Sequence of Scores sheet. Count the number of times *CON* occurs.

section can be completed in eight easy steps. The directions for each of these steps rely on the transparency template and numbering system used on the upper section of the Structural Summary form. Place your photocopied transparency from Appendix 5a on top of the uppersection of the Structural Summary to aid you in scoring. For help with the more complex equations found in the lower section of the Structural Summary, place your second photocopied transparency from Appendix 5b on the lower section of the Structural Summary. The transparencies show our numbering system for both the upper and the lower section.

There is an Exner formula for each score in the lower section, which the examiner will find in the Exner's Comprehensive System book (Exner, 1993). Our template, numbering system, and the Shortcuts found in this chapter will save time and eliminate the common adding mistakes made by first-time examiners and infrequent users. The Shortcuts rely on the template and numbering system. You need only to look on the upper section of the Structural Summary to find the appropriate numbers, which are then plugged into the formulas. When a score from one lower section equation is used in a second

Table 4.12 Special Scores Raw Sum6 and Weighted Sum 6

Variable Name	Variable Number	Directions for Scoring
Raw Sum6	108	Total the number of responses of the special scores: 98 + 99 + 100 + 101 + 102 + 103 + 104 + 105 + 106 + 107
Wgtd Sum6 (Wsum6)	109	Multiply the special scores by the required weights, then tally for a total: 1*98 + 2*99 + 2*100 + 4*101 + 3*102 + 6*103 + 4*104 + 7*105 + 5*106 + 7*107

Table 4.13 Special Scores AB through PSV

Variable Name	Variable Number	Directions for Scoring
AB	110	Look under the Special Scores column of the Sequence of Scores sheet for *AB* responses. Count the number of times this occurs.
AG	111	Same as 110, but look for *AG* responses. Count the number of times this occurs.
CFB	112	Same as 110, but look for *CFB* responses. Count the number of times this occurs.
COP	113	Same as 110, but look for *COP* responses. Count the number of times this occurs.
CP	114	Same as 110, but look for *CP* responses. Count the number of times this occurs.
MOR	115	Same as 110, but look for *MOR* responses. Count the number of times this occurs.
PER	116	Same as 110, but look for *PER* responses. Count the number of times this occurs.
PSV	117	Same as 110, but look for *PSV* responses. Count the number of times this occurs.

lower section equation, the score from the first is referred to in brackets (e.g., {L.3.4}, meaning use the score in the lower half of the Structural Summary form, L.3.4). We've included helpful hints for individual formulas when appropriate. In summary, within each section, you will find Exner's formulas, Shortcuts using our template and numbering system, and helpful hints.

Rapid Reference 4.3

Seven Sections of the Lower Half of the Structural Summary Form

1. Core
2. Ideation
3. Affect
4. Mediation
5. Processing
6. Interpersonal
7. Self-perception

Before beginning the lower section of the Structural Summary, note the rules for filling in scores on the lower section in Don't Forget 4.1. Caution 4.2 describes common errors in scoring the lower section that should be avoided.

Core Section (L.1)

The first area of the lower half of the scoring form is the Core Section and has 16 entries (R, L, EB, EA, Ebper, eb, es, D, Adj. es, Adj. D, FM, C', T, m, V, Y). For new examiners, this can be the most difficult section to complete. One of the most confusing aspects of Exner's equations is the distinction between Sum and Sum All. See Don't Forget 4.2 for explanation.

R: Total Number of Responses (L.1.1)

R is a count of all the responses, each separate answer, that the examinee gave during the administration.

Hint: To find this score, first look at the Sequence of Scores sheet. Second, find the column labeled Resp. No. Third, look for the last number listed at the bottom of the column; it will be the highest number. Fourth, write this number down to the right of R.

Rapid Reference 4.4

Six Special Indices Scores

1. Schizophrenia Index (SCZI)
2. Depression Index (DEPI)
3. Coping Deficit Index (CDI)
4. Suicide Constellation (S-Con)
5. Hypervigilance (HVI)
6. Obsessive Style (OBS)

L: Lambda (L.1.2)

Lambda is the proportion of pure F that occurred in the record.

Formula:

$$L = \frac{F \text{ (number of responses having only pure F determinants)}}{R-F \text{ (total } R \text{ minus pure } F \text{ determinants)}}$$

Hint: Use the same number from R {L.1.1}, listed in the previous entry.

Shortcut:

$$L = \frac{\boxed{40}}{R \{\text{from L.1.1}\} - \boxed{40}}$$

EB — Erlebnistypus (L.1.3)

Erlebnistypus is a ratio comparing the sum of human movement (Sum M) to the Weighted sum of color responses (WSumC).

Formula: Sum M:WsumC
{WSumC = (.5)*FC + (1.0)*CF + (1.5)*C}

Hint: 1. This score is a ratio. The colon between the two sums means create a ratio between the two scores.

2. *Sum* refers to Blends and Singles of only that determinant.

Shortcut: $\boxed{18}$ + $\boxed{17}$ {look for only individual *M*'s}: (.5)*($\boxed{21}$ + $\boxed{17}$ {look for *FC*'s}) + (1.0)*($\boxed{22}$+$\boxed{17}$ {look for *CF*'s}) + (1.5)*($\boxed{23}$ + $\boxed{17}$ {look for *C*'s})

EA — Experience Actual (L.1.4)

Experience Actual is the sum of human movement and weighted color responses.

Formula: Sum M + WsumC

Hint: This score adds both sides of the ratio together from EB {L.1.3}.

Shortcut: $\boxed{18}$ + $\boxed{17}$ {look for only individual *M*'s} + (.5)*($\boxed{21}$ + $\boxed{17}$ {look for *FC*'s}) + (1.0)*($\boxed{22}$ + $\boxed{17}$ {look for *CF*'s}) + (1.5)*($\boxed{23}$ + $\boxed{17}$ {look for *C*'s})

EBPer — EB Pervasive (L.1.5)

EB Pervasive is a ratio that is calculated when there is a marked style indicated in EB {L.1.3} (see Caution 4.3). It is the proportion of the sum of human movement to the sum of weighted color response or the sum of weighted color response to the sum of human movement.

Formula: $\dfrac{\text{Sum M}}{\text{WSumC}}$ or $\dfrac{\text{WsumC}}{\text{Sum M}}$

Hint: 1. The final score can be either the first equation or the second equation. The rule for EBPer is that the examiner must divide the larger number by the smaller number.

2. Calculate by dividing the larger number by the smaller number in EB {L.1.3}. Use both Sum M and WSumC from EB.

Eb — Experience Base (L.1.6)

Experience Base is the relationship comparing all nonhuman movement to all shading and all achromatic color.

> # DON'T FORGET 4.2
>
> ## Sum versus Sum All Determinants
>
> Sum refers to counting up both Blends and Singles of *only* that specific determinant.
>
> Example:
>
> Sum *M* (Human Movement) = *M* under Singles + *M* under Blends (do not include *FM* or *m*).
>
> *Sum All* refers to counting up both Blends and Singles of all combinations of a determinant.
>
> Example:
>
> Sum all *C'* = *C'* under Singles and Blends + *C'F* under Singles and Blends + *FC'* under Singles and Blends.

Formula: Sum *FM* + *m*:Sum all *C'* + all *T* + all *Y* + all *V*

Hint: 1. Sum All means add all combinations of that determinant in Blends and Singles.

2. Jump ahead and complete {L.1.11} to {L.1.16}, then use the numbers for this equation.

Shortcut: ([19] + [17] {look only for *FM*'s}) +([20]+[17] {look only for *m*'s}): ([25] + [26] + [27] + [17] {look for all combinations of *C'*}) + ([28]+[29]+[30]+[17] {look for all combinations of *T*}) + ([34]+[35]+[36] + [17] {look for all combinations of *Y*}) + ([31]+[32] +[33]+[17] {look for all combinations of *V*})

Es — Experienced Stimulation (L.1.7)

Experienced Stimulation is a derivation of eb {L.1.6}. It is the sum of all nonhuman movement, all shading and all achromatic color.

Formula: Sum $FM + m$ + all C' + all T + all Y + all V

Hint: Use the numbers from eb {L.1.6}, but add the left and the right side of the ratio together.

Shortcut: ($\boxed{19} + \boxed{17}$ {look only for FM's}) + ($\boxed{20} + \boxed{17}$ {look only for m's}) + ($\boxed{25} + \boxed{26} + \boxed{27} + \boxed{17}$ {look for all combinations of C'}) + ($\boxed{28} + \boxed{29} + \boxed{30} + \boxed{17}$ {look for all combinations of T}) + ($\boxed{34} + \boxed{35} + \boxed{36} + \boxed{17}$ {look for all combinations of Y}) + ($\boxed{31} + \boxed{32} + \boxed{33} + \boxed{17}$ {look for all combinations of V})

D — The D Score (L.1.8)

The D score is a scaled difference score based on the sum of human movement and weighted color response minus the sum of nonhuman movement, all shading, and all achromatic color.

Formula: Raw Scale Difference = EA−es

Hint: 1. Include a plus or minus sign in the final score because when subtracting *es* in the equation the final entry could be a negative or positive number.

2. The D Score Conversion Table is based on a standard deviation rounded to 2.5; so for every 2.5 difference between EA and es, the D score will increase or decrease by 1.0.

Shortcut: There are two steps for this entry.

1. Calculate EA−es or {L.1.4} − {L.1.7}.
2. Look up the Scaled Difference score on the D Score Conversion Table in Rapid

CAUTION 4.5

When to Calculate EBPer

EBPer is calculated only when there is a "marked style" indicated in the EB {L.1.3}. This is true when

1. value of EA is 10.0 or less.

2. one side of EB is at least 2 points greater than the other side.

3. value of EA is more than 10.0 *and* one side of the EB is at least 2.5 points greater than the other side.

Reference 4.5 or in Table 29 on page 185 of Exner (volume 1, 1993).

3. If the D score is not listed in the Conversion Table, you can expand the scale in two-degree increments. For example, +20.5 to +22.5 is a D score of +8 and so on.

Adj es —Adjusted es (L.1.9)

Adjusted es is a derivation of es, Experienced Stimulation {L.1.7} (the sum of nonhuman movement, all shading, and all achromatic color) subtracting the sum of all but one nonhuman movement, as well as subtracting all but one diffuse shading.

Formula: es − (all but 1 m) − (all but 1 Y)

Hint: Don't forget to subtract one m, from all m's and one Y from all Y's before subtracting m's and y's from es. If there are no m's and no y's then subtract zero.

Shortcut: es {L.1.7} − (⬚20⬚ + ⬚17⬚ {look only for m's} − 1 m) − (⬚34⬚ + ⬚35⬚ + ⬚36⬚ + ⬚17⬚ {look for all combinations of Y} − 1Y)

Adj D —Adjusted D (L.1.10)

Adjusted D is Experience Actual minus Adjusted Experienced Stimulation. The numbers from the previous equations are used to tally the score.

Formula: EA − Adj es

Hint: Use the D Score Conversion Table from Rapid Reference 4.5.

Shortcut: There are two steps for this entry.

1. Calculate EA − Adj es or {L.1.4}−{L.1.9}.
2. Look up the Scaled Difference score on the D Score Conversion Table, as done in {L.1.8}.

FM (L.1.11)

This score is a tally of all responses with an animal movement determinant. There are many scores similar to this one on the lower section of the Structural

Summary. All that is required is to add up the number of times a coded variable appears in the administration. Often times, an examiner has already tallied the score while calculating the more complex equations earlier in the section. In fact, the more experienced examiner might choose to fill in the scores for each section in a different order; first completing the simple tallies, then using the scores for the more complex equations.

Hint: Use the frequency data from the Single Determinants column on the upper portion of the Structural Summary form. Do the same for the following five formulas.

Shortcut: $\boxed{19} + \boxed{17}$ {look only for FM's}

C' (L.1.12)

This score is a tally of all responses with an achromatic color determinant, including C', FC', and $C'F$.

Shortcut: $\boxed{25} + \boxed{26} + \boxed{27} + \boxed{17}$ {look for C''s, FC''s and $C'F$'s}

T (L.1.13)

This score is a tally of all responses with a texture response, including T, FT, and TF.

Shortcut: $\boxed{28} + \boxed{29} + \boxed{30} + \boxed{17}$ {look for T's, FT's, and TF's}

m (L.1.14)

This score is a tally of all responses with an inanimate movement determinant.

Shortcut: $\boxed{20} + \boxed{17}$ {look only for m's}

V (L.1.15)

V is a tally of all responses with a vista determinant including V, FV, VF.

Shortcut: $\boxed{31} + \boxed{32} + \boxed{33} + \boxed{17}$ {look for V's, FV's, and VF's}

Y (L.1.16)

Y is a tally of all responses with a shading determinant including Y, FY, and YF.

Shortcut: $\boxed{34} + \boxed{35} + \boxed{36} + \boxed{17}$ {look for Y's, FY's, and YF's}

≡ Rapid Reference 4.5

D Score Conversion Table

Look under the Value (of EA−es) column for the examinee's EA−es or EA−Adj es score. Follow along the row to the next number under the D Score column. This is the examinee's D score. For example, an EA−es score of +4 would be converted to a D score of +1.

Value of (EA-es)	D Score
+18.0 to +20.0	+7
+15.5 to +17.5	+6
+13.0 to +15.0	+5
+10.5 to +12.5	+4
+8.0 to +10.0	+3
+5.5 to +7.5	+2
+3.0 to +5.0	+1
−2.5 to +2.5	0
−3.0 to − 5.0	−1
−5.0 to −7.5	−2
−8.0 to − 10.0	−3
−10.5 to − 12.5	−4
−13.0 to − 15.0	−5
−15.5 to − 17.5	−6
−18.0 to − 20.0	−7

Note. Modified from Exner (1993) Table 29, p. 185.

Ideation Section (L.2)

The second area of the lower half of the Structural Summary form is the Ideation Section. There are eight entries in this section (*a:p*, *Ma:Mp*, 2*AB* + (*Art* +*Ay*), *M*−, Sum6, WSum6, Lvl-2, Mnone), four frequencies, two ratios, and one equation.

a:p — Active:Passive Ratio (L.2.1)

The Active:Passive Ratio is a relationship of active and passive movement determinants. The active movements are on the left side of the ratio and the passive movements are on the right.

Formula: $M^a + FM^a + m^a : M^p + FM^p + m^p$

Shortcut: 1. Go back to the Determinants and Form Quality column on the Sequence of Scores sheet.

2. Look for any *M, FM,* and *m* followed by a superscript *a, p,* or *a–p.*

3. Count and total each and put into ratio form. (*Important Note:* Movement determinants (*M, FM, m*) with an *a–p* superscript are added to both sides of the ratio.)

4. Put the active movement and the active-passive movement on the left side of the ratio and the passive movement and the active-passive movement on the right side of the ratio.

Ma:Mp — M Active:Passive Ratio (L.2.2)

This ratio is similar to the last, however only human movement is examined. In this equation, all the active human movement is on the left side and all the passive human movement is on the right.

Hint: This formula includes only human movement, *M.*

Shortcut: 1. Go back to the Determinants and Form Quality column on the Sequence of Scores sheet.

2. Look for any *M* followed by a superscript a, p, or a–p.

3. Count and total each and put into ratio form. (*Important Note:* *M*'s with a superscript a–p are added to both sides of the ratio.)

4. Put the active movement and the active-passive movements on the left side of the ratio and the passive movement and the active-passive movements on the right side of the ratio.

2AB + (Art + Ay) — The Intellectualization Index (L.2.3)

This equation is often referred to as the Intellectualization Index. It is composed of all abstract content special scores multiplied by two, plus all art and anthropology content scores.

Hint: Both primary and secondary contents are included in the equation (both numbers that are separated by a comma for $\boxed{71}$ and $\boxed{72}$).

Shortcut: $2 * \boxed{110} + (\boxed{71} + \boxed{72})$

M – (L.2.4)

This score is a tally of all responses with human movement determinants and form quality minus (distorted or unrealistic form in the response).

Hint: Use the frequency data from the upper section of the Structural Summary form. Do the same for the following four formulas ({L.2.6} also includes a simple calculation.)

Shortcut: $\boxed{54}$

Sum6 (L.2.5)

Raw Sum6 is an equation tallying six special scores that concern unusual verbalizations. They include deviant verbalizations (*DV* and *DR*), inappropriate combinations (*INCOM*, *FABCOM* and *CONTAM*) and inappropriate logic response (*ALOG*).

Shortcut: $\boxed{108}$

Lvl-2 (L.2.6)

Level 2 is an equation of all level 2 special scores including deviant verbalizations lvl-2, deviant responses lvl-2, incongruous combinations lvl-2, and fabulized combination lvl-2 combinations.

Shortcut: $\boxed{99} + \boxed{101} + \boxed{103} + \boxed{105}$

WSum6 (L.2.7)

Weighted Sum6 is an equation tallying the same special scores from Raw Sum6 {L.2.5} but adding specific weights to each variable for a level 1 or level 2 response. The abbreviation is also seen as Wgtd Sum6.

Shortcut: $\boxed{109}$

Mnone (L.2.8)

Form Quality Human Movement None is a tally of all responses that include a human movement and no Form Quality.

Shortcut: $\boxed{55}$

Affect Section (L.3)

The third area of the lower half of the summary is the Affect Section. There are seven entries in this section (Sum*FC*:Sum*CF* + *C*, Pure *C*, Sum*C*': WsumC, Afr, *S*, Blends:R, *CP*), three frequencies, three ratios, and one equation.

Sum FC:Sum CF + C—Form–Color Ratio (L.3.1)

This ratio focuses on color and form determinant usage. All form-color response determinants are on the left and all color-form and color naming response determinants are on the right side of the ratio.

Hint: Equation includes color naming, *Cn*.

Shortcut: $\boxed{21}$ + $\boxed{17}$ {look for *FC*'s} : $\boxed{22}$ + $\boxed{23}$ + $\boxed{24}$ + $\boxed{17}$ {look for *CF*'s, *C*'s, *Cn*'s}

Pure C (L.3.2)

This score is a tally of all responses with a pure color determination.

Shortcut: $\boxed{23}$ + $\boxed{17}$ {look for *C*'s}

SumC':WsumC—Constriction Ratio (L.3.3)

This ratio, sometimes called the Constriction Ratio, compares all achromatic color responses to the weighted sum of chromatic color responses.

Shortcut: 25 + 26 + 27 + 17 {look for *C*'s, *C'F*s, *FC*'s}: right side of ratio {from entry L.1.3}

Hint: Not all computer-generated Structural Summaries include this variable.

Afr—Affective Ratio (L.3.4)

This score, sometimes called the Affective Ratio, compares the total number of responses to the last three cards to the total number of responses to the first seven cards.

Formula: $$\frac{\text{Number Responses to Cards VIII + IX + X}}{\text{Number Responses to Cards I + II + III + IV + V + VI + VII}}$$

Hint: 1. Each Response is separated by a decimal point for scores $\boxed{88}$ through $\boxed{97}$.

2. The computer-generated Structural Summaries do not include the Approach Summary, scores $\boxed{88}$ – $\boxed{97}$ on the upper section, instead they list the Suicide Constellation Index. Instead refer to the Sequence of Scores sheet for the number of responses to each card.

Shortcut: $$\frac{\text{Number of Responses to } \boxed{95} + \boxed{96} + \boxed{97}}{\text{Number of Responses to } \boxed{88} + \boxed{89} + \boxed{90} + \boxed{91} + \boxed{92} + \boxed{93} + \boxed{94}}$$

S (L.3.5)

S is a tally of space location responses.

Shortcut: $\boxed{8}$

Blends — R Complexity Ratio (L.3.6)

This score, often called the Complexity Ratio, compares the total number of responses that include multiple determinants (blends) to the total number of responses given during the administration.

Hint: "Total number of blends" refers to the number of rows hand-written under "Blends."

Shortcut: Total number of blends under $\boxed{17}$:Total number of responses or R {from L.1.1}.

CP (L.3.7)

CP is a tally of all color projection special score responses.

Shortcut: $\boxed{114}$

Mediation Section (L.4)

The fourth area of the lower half of the summary is the Mediation Section. There are six entries in this section (P, X+%, F+%, X–%, S–%, Xu%), one frequency, and five percentages.

P (L.4.1)

P is a tally of all popular responses.

Shortcut: Go back to Sequence of Scores sheet and count the number of P's in the Pops column.

X+% — Conventional Form (L.4.2)

X+% is called Conventional Form and examines the number of Form Quality responses that are either superior-overelaborated or ordinary compared to the total number of responses given during the administration.

Formula: $\dfrac{\text{Sum FQx + and o}}{R}$

Shortcut: $\dfrac{\boxed{42} + \boxed{43}}{R \{\text{from L.1.1}\}}$

F+% — Conventional Pure Form (L.4.3)

F+% is called Conventional Pure Form and examines the total number of Form Quality responses that are either superior-overelaborated or ordinary when the determinant pure form is recorded compared to the total number of pure form responses.

Formula: $\dfrac{\text{Sum } F + \text{and o}}{\text{Sum } F}$

Shortcut: $\dfrac{\boxed{47} + \boxed{48}}{\boxed{47} + \boxed{48} + \boxed{49} + \boxed{50}}$

X–% — Distorted Form (L.4.4)

X–% is called Distorted Form and examines the total number of Form Quality responses that are minus compared to the total number of responses given during the administration.

Formula: $\dfrac{\text{Sum FQx}-}{R}$

Shortcut: $\dfrac{\boxed{45}}{R\ \{\text{from L.1.1}\}}$

S–% — White Space Distribution (L.4.5)

S–% is called White Space Distribution and examines the number of Form Quality responses that are minus that also include space location compared to the total number of Form Quality responses that are minus.

Formula: $\dfrac{\text{Sum SQ}-}{\text{Sum FQx}-}$

Shortcut: $\dfrac{\boxed{59}}{\boxed{45}}$

Xu% — Unusual Form (L.4.6)

Xu% is called Unusual form and examines the number of Form Quality responses that are unusual compared to the total number of responses given during the administration.

Formula: $\dfrac{\text{Sum FQxu}}{R}$

Shortcut: $\dfrac{\boxed{44}}{R\ \{\text{from L.1.1}\}}$

Processing Section (L.5)

The fifth area of the lower half of the summary is the Processing Section. There are six entries in this section (Zf, Zd, $W{:}D{:}Dd$, $W{:}M$, DQ+, DQv), three frequencies, two ratios, and one difference score.

Zf (L.5.1)

The Z frequency score is the number of responses that have a Z score.

Shortcut: $\boxed{1}$

Zd—Processing Efficiency (L.5.2)

Processing Efficiency is a difference score that tallies all the Z scores and subtracts a weighted sum of all the Z scores.

Formula: ZSum – Zest

Shortcut: $\boxed{2} - \boxed{3}$

W:D:Dd—Economy Index (L.5.3)

The Economy Index is a ratio of the number of whole location responses to the number of common detail location responses to the number of unusual detail location responses.

Hint: The total number of *W* responses on the left, the total number of *D* responses in the middle, and the total number of *Dd* responses on the right.

Shortcut: $\boxed{4} : \boxed{6} : \boxed{7}$

W:M—Aspirational Ratio (L.5.4)

The Aspirational Ratio is a ratio of the number of whole location responses to the number of human movement determinant responses.

Hint: 1. Do not reduce ratio.

2. The total number of *W* responses on the right and the total number of *M* responses on the left.

Shortcut: $\boxed{4} : \boxed{18} + \boxed{17}$ { look for *M*'s}

DQ+ (L.5.5)

This score is a tally of the total number of Developmental Quality Synthesized responses.

Shortcut: $\boxed{9}$

DQv (L.5.6)

This score is a tally of the total number of Developmental Quality Vague responses.

Shortcut: $\boxed{12}$

Interpersonal Section (L.6)

The sixth area of the lower half of the summary is the Interpersonal Section. There are seven entries in this section (COP, AG, Food, Isolate/R, H:(H) + Hd + (Hd), (H) + (Hd):(A) + (Ad), H + A:Hd + Ad), three frequencies, and four ratios.

COP (L.6.1)

This score is a tally of the total number of cooperative movement special score responses.

Shortcut: $\boxed{113}$

AG (L.6.2)

This score is a tally of the total number of aggressive movement special score responses.

Shortcut: $\boxed{111}$

Food (L.6.3)

This score is a tally of the total number of food content responses.

Formula: Fd

Hint: Include both primary and secondary content scores, the numbers separated by a comma. Do the same for the next four scores in this section.

Shortcut: $\boxed{78}$

Isolate/R—Isolation Index (L.6.4)

This equation, called the Isolation Index, compares five content responses—botany, clouds, geology, landscape, and nature—to the total number of responses given during the administration.

Formula: $\dfrac{Bt + 2Cl + Ge + Ls + 2Na}{R}$

Shortcut: $\dfrac{\boxed{74} + (2*\boxed{76}) + \boxed{80} + \boxed{82} + (2*\boxed{83})}{R\{\text{from L.1.1}\}}$

H:(H) + Hd + (Hd)—Interpersonal Interest (L.6.5)

This ratio, called Interpersonal Interest, contrasts all whole human content responses to all whole human content responses that are fictional or mythological and all human detail content responses that are nonfictional, fictional, or mythological.

Shortcut: $\boxed{61}:\boxed{62}+\boxed{63}+\boxed{64}$

(H) + (Hd):(A) + (Ad) (L.6.6)

This ratio compares all whole human and human detail content responses that are fictional or mythological to all whole or animal detail content responses that are fictional or mythological.

Shortcut: $\boxed{62}+\boxed{64}:\boxed{67}+\boxed{69}$

H + A:Hd + Ad (L.6.7)

This ratio compares all whole human and whole animal content responses to all human detail and animal detail human responses.

Shortcut: $\boxed{61}+\boxed{66}:\boxed{63}+\boxed{68}$

Self-Perception Section (L.7)

The seventh area of the lower half of the summary is the Self-Perception Section. There are five entries in this section (3r + (2)/R, *Fr + rF*, *FD*, *An + Xy*, *MOR*), four frequencies, and one equation.

3r +(2)/R—Egocentricity Index (L.7.1)

This equation, called the Egocentricity Index, examines the total number of reflection and pair determinant responses to the total number of responses given during administration.

Formula:
$$\frac{3x(Fr + rF) + Sum(2)}{R}$$

Shortcut:
$$\frac{3*(\boxed{37}+\boxed{38}+\boxed{17}\ \{\text{look for } Fr\text{'s and } rF\text{'s}\})+\boxed{41}+\boxed{17}\ \{\text{look for } (2)\text{s, but there should not be any}\}}{R\ \{\text{from L.1.1}\}}$$

Fr + rF (L.7.2)

This score is a tally of the total number of form-reflection and reflection-form determinant responses.

Shortcut: $\boxed{37}$ + $\boxed{38}$ + $\boxed{17}$ {look for *Fr*'s and *rF*'s}

FD (L.7.3)

This score is a tally of the total number of form based dimensional determinant responses.

Shortcut: $\boxed{39}$ + $\boxed{17}$ {look for *FD*'s}

An + Xy (L.7.4)

This score is a tally of the total number of anatomy and X-ray content responses.

Hint: Include both primary and secondary contents, the numbers separated by a comma.

Shortcut: $\boxed{70}$ + $\boxed{86}$

MOR (L.7.5)

This score is a tally of the total number of morbid content special score responses.

Shortcut: $\boxed{115}$

Special Indices (L.8)

There are six Special Indices listed on the last line of the bottom section of the Structural Summary form. They are completed using the information from the Constellations Worksheet. The six special indices are S-Con, measuring suicide potential; DEPI, a depression index; HVI, a hypervigilance index; SCZI, a schizophrenia index; CDI, a coping deficit index; and OBS, an obsessive style index (see Rapid Reference 4.4 earlier in this chapter).

The check boxes for each index are on the bottom of the Structural Summary form and are checked if the index meets criteria, based on the worksheet (see Rapid Reference 4.6). It is important to note that the Constellation Worksheet scores are in a different order than on the Structural

Summary form (see Caution 4.4). Once again the shortcuts use the template transparency and our numbering system to translate the formulas. Note that several of the Shortcuts use scores from the lower half of the Structural Summary form. Don't Forget 4.3 lists instructions for scoring special indices.

≡ Rapid Reference 4.6

When an Index Is Positive

"The index is positive when five conditions are true" means that an index meets criteria when five "greater than" and "less than" statements are mathematically accurate. In those cases, the index is considered an indication of that psychological component or style.

S-Constellation: Suicide Potential (L.8.1)

In the Suicide Potential Constellation there are twelve possible conditions. The index is positive if eight or more conditions are true (see Caution 4.5). However, do not use this index for examinees under 14 years of age.

$FV + VF + V + FD > 2$ (L.8.1.a)

Shortcut: $\boxed{31} + \boxed{32} + \boxed{33} + \boxed{39} + \boxed{17}$ {look for FV's, VF's, V's, and FD's} > 2

Color-Shading Blends > 0 (L.8.1.b)

Shortcut: Look under the Blends column and determine if Color and Shading were used in the same response (the same row, separated by a period).

Count the number of times this happens. (Color responses include C, CF, FC, Cn, C', $C'F$, FC', and Shading responses include T, TF, FT, V, VF, FV, Y, YF, FY.)

$3r + (2) / R < .31$ or $> .44$ (L.8.1c)

Shortcut: (Entry from L.7.1 < .31) or (Entry from L.7.1 > .44)

CAUTION 4.4

Order of Special Indices

The Special Indices are in a different order on the Constellations Worksheet than they are on the Structural Summary form. This Essentials book follows the order on the Constellation Worksheet.

MOR > 3 (L.8.1.d)

Shortcut: $\boxed{115} > 3$

Zd > +3.5 or < −3.5 (L.8.1.e)

Shortcut: (Entry from L.5.2 > +3.5) or (Entry from L.5.2 < −3.5)

es > EA (L.8.1.f)

Shortcut: Entry from L.1.7 > Entry from L.1.4

CF + C > FC (L.8.1.g)

Shortcut: $\boxed{22} + \boxed{23} + \boxed{17}$ {look for *CF*'s and *C*'s} $> \boxed{21} + \boxed{17}$ {look for *FC*'s}

X+% < .70 (L.8.1.h)

Shortcut: Entry from L.4.2 < .70

DON'T FORGET 4.3

Scoring Special Indices

- At the bottom of the Structural Summary form, there are six boxes, one each for the six Special Indices. Check the appropriate box when an index is positive (meets criteria).
- For SCZI, DEPI, CDI, and S-Con, the total number of positive conditions should be written in after the equal sign.
- For HVI and OBS, the words *no* or *yes*, as appropriate, should be written in after the equal sign.

S > 3 (L.8.1.i)

Shortcut: $\boxed{8} > 3$

P < 3 or P > 8 (L.8.1.j)

Shortcut: (Entry from L.4.3 < 3) *or* (Entry from L.4.3 > 8)

Pure H < 2 (L.8.1.k)

Hint: Include both primary and secondary contents.

Shortcut: $\boxed{61} < 2$

R < 17 (L.8.1.l)

Shortcut: Entry from L.1.1 < 17

DEPI: Depression Index (L.8.2)

In the Depression Index there are seven possible conditions. This index is positive if five or more conditions are true. See Caution 4.6 for examinees under 14 years of age.

(FV + VF + V > 0) or (FD > 2) (L.8.2.a)

Shortcut: ($\boxed{31}$ + $\boxed{32}$ + $\boxed{33}$ + $\boxed{17}$ {look for FV's, VF's and V's} > 0) or ($\boxed{39}$ + $\boxed{17}$ {look for FD's} > 2)

(Color-Shading Blends > 0) or (S > 2) (L.8.2.b)

Shortcut: (Entry from L.8.1.b >0) or ($\boxed{8}$ > 2)

Either (3r + (2)/R > .44) and (Fr + rF = 0) or (3r + (2)/R < .33) (L.8.2.c)

Shortcut: [(Entry from L.7.1 > .44) and (Entry from L.7.2 = 0)] or (L.7.1 < .33)

(Afr < .46) or (Blends < 4) (L.8.2.d)

Shortcut: (Entry from L.3.4 < .46) or (Left side of ratio from L.3.6)

(Sum Shading > Fm + m) or (Sum C' > 2) (L.8.2.e)

Shortcut: ($\boxed{28}$ + $\boxed{29}$ + $\boxed{30}$ + $\boxed{31}$ + $\boxed{32}$ + $\boxed{33}$ + $\boxed{34}$ + $\boxed{35}$ + $\boxed{36}$ + $\boxed{17}$ {look for all T, FT, TF, V, FV, VF, Y, FY, YF} > $\boxed{19}$ + $\boxed{20}$ + $\boxed{17}$ {look for all FM, m} or ($\boxed{27}$ + $\boxed{17}$ {look for only C'} > 2)

(MOR > 2) or (2xAB + Art + Ay > 3) (L.8.2.f)

Shortcut: ($\boxed{115}$ > 2) or (Entry from L.2.3 > 3)

(COP < 2) or ([Bt + 2xCl + Ge + Ls +2xNa]/R >.24) (L.8.2.g)

Shortcut: ($\boxed{113}$ < 2) or (Entry from L.6.4 > .24)

HVI: Hypervigilance Index (L.8.3)

In the Hypervigilance Index there are eight possible conditions. Index is positive if condition 1 (L.8.3.a.) is true and at least four of the others are true (L.8.3.b through L.8.3.h).

CAUTION 4.5

S-Constellation

This index is positive if eight or more conditions are true; however, false negatives are possible. In other words, an examinee can be suicidal even if fewer than eight variables are checked.

FT + TF + T = 0 (L.8.3.a)

Shortcut: $\boxed{28}$ + $\boxed{29}$ + $\boxed{30}$ + $\boxed{17}$ {look for all *FT, TF,* and *T*} = 0

Zf > 12 (L.8.3.b)

Shortcut: $\boxed{1}$ > 12

Zd > +3.5 (L.8.3.c)

Shortcut: Entry for L.5.2 > +3.5

S > 3 (L.8.3.d)

Shortcut: $\boxed{8}$ > 3

H + (H) + Hd + (Hd) > 6 (L.8.3.e)

Hint: Include both primary and secondary content scores. Do the same for the following three scores.

Shortcut: $\boxed{61}$ + $\boxed{62}$ + $\boxed{63}$ + $\boxed{64}$ > 6

(H) + (A) + (Hd) + (Ad) > 3 (L.8.3.f)

Shortcut: $\boxed{62}$ + $\boxed{67}$ + $\boxed{64}$ + $\boxed{69}$ > 3

H + A:Hd + Ad < 4:1 (L.8.3.g)

Shortcut: Entry from L.6.7 is less than a 4 to 1 ratio

Cg > 3 (L.8.3.h)

Shortcut: $\boxed{75}$ > 3

SCZI: Schizophrenia Index (L.8.4)

In the Schizophrenia Index there are six possible conditions. The index is positive if four or more conditions are true. See Caution 4.5 earlier in this chapter for examinees under 14 years of age.

Either (X+% < .61) and (S–% < .41) Or (X+% < .50) (L.8.4.a)

Shortcut: [(Entry from L.4.2 < .61) and (Entry from L.4.5 < .41)] or (Entry from L.4.2 < .50)

X–% > .29 (L.8.4.b)

Shortcut: Entry from L.4.4 > .29

(FQ–> = FQu) Or (FQ- > FQo + FQ+) (L.8.4.c)

Hint: ">=" means "greater than or equal to"

Shortcut: ([45] >= [44]) or [[45] > ([43] + [42])]

(Sum Level 2 Special Scoring > 1) and (FAB 2 > 0) (L.8.4.d)

Shortcut: ([99] + [101] + [103] + [105] > 1) and ([105] > 0)

Either (Raw Sum 6 Special Scoring > 6) Or (Weighted Sum 6 Special Scoring >17) (L.8.4.e)

Shortcut: ([108] > 6) or ([109] > 17)

(M–> 1) or (X–% > .40) (L.8.4.f)

Shortcut: ([54] > 1) or (Entry from L.4.4 > .40)

CDI: Coping Deficit Index (L.8.5)

In the Coping Deficit Index there are five possible conditions. The index is positive if four or five conditions are true.

CAUTION 4.6

Constellation Worksheet and Examinees under 14 Years of Age

- For DEPI and SCZI indices, cut-offs should be adjusted to exceed +/– Standard Deviation for
  1. RawSum6 (Sum6)
  2. Wgtd Sum6 (WSum6)
  3. (Egocentricity Index) $3r + (2)/R$
  4. X+%
- For S-Con, or Suicide Constellation, a positive index is based on adult data and should not be applied to younger examinees.

(EA < 6) or *(Adj D < 0) (L.8.5.a)*

Shortcut: (Entry from L.1.4 < 6) or (Entry from L.1.10 < 0)

(COP < 2) and *(AG < 2) (L.8.5.b)*

Shortcut: ($\boxed{113}$ < 2) and ($\boxed{111}$ < 2)

(Weighted Sum C < 2.5) or *(Afr < .46) (L.8.5.c)*

Shortcut: (Right side of ratio from L.1.3) or (Entry from L.3.4 < .46)

(Passive > Active + 1) or *(Pure H < 2) (L.8.5.d)*

Shortcut: (The right side of the ratio from L.2.1 > The left side of the ratio from L.2.1 + 1) or ($\boxed{61}$ < 2)

Either: (Sum T > 1) or *(Isolate/R > .24)* or *(Food > 0) (L.8.5.e)*

Shortcut: ($\boxed{30}$ + $\boxed{17}$ {look only for T} > 1) or (Entry from L.6.4 > .24) or ($\boxed{78}$ > 0)

OBS: Obsessive Style Index (L.8.6)

In the Obsessive Style Index there are five possible conditions. The index is positive if one or more of the following statements are true:
1. conditions 1–5 (L.8.6a,b,c,d,e) are all true,
2. two or more of Conditions 1–4 (L.8.6a,b,c,d) are true *and* FQ+ > 3,

   Shortcut: $\boxed{42}$ > 3

3. three or more of Conditions 1–5 (L.8.6a,b,c,d,e) are true and X+% > .89,

   Shortcut: Entry from L.4.2 > .89

4. or (FQ+ > 3) and (X+% > .89).

   Shortcut: $\boxed{42}$ > 3 and Entry from L.4.2 > .89

Dd > 3 (L.8.6.a)

   Shortcut: $\boxed{7}$ > 3

Zf > 12 (L.8.6.b)

   Shortcut: $\boxed{1}$ > 12

Zd > + 3.0 (L.8.6.c)

Shortcut: Entry from L.5.2 > 3.0

Populars > 7 (L.8.6.d)

Shortcut: Entry from L.4.1 > 7

FQ+ > 1 (L.8.6.e)

Shortcut: $\boxed{42}$ > 1

🦅 TEST YOURSELF 🦅

1. **Do not divide and reduce equations with a numerator and a denominator.** True or False?
2. **Do not reduce ratio equations.** True or False?
3. **Everything you need to fill in the lower half of the Structural Summary form is on the upper half of the Structural Summary form.** True or False?
4. **What is the difference between *Sum All* and *Sum*?**
5. **How do you find a *D* score?**
6. **How many true answers are needed to get a Special Index score?**
   (a) It requires 4 or 5 true answers, depending on the Index.
   (b) Every Special Index has its own number of true answers needed.
   (c) At least half of the answers need to be true.
   (d) All of them need to be true.
7. **Where would an examiner look to calculate *Pure C* on the lower half of the Structural Summary form?**
8. **What does *R* mean, and how does an examiner calculate it?**

Answers: 1. False. Reduce the division equations; 2. True. Do not reduce ratio equations; 3. False. For some entries the examiner needs to go back to the Sequence of Scores sheet. Additionally, in order to the complete the Special Indices, the examiner needs to fill in the Constellation Worksheet; 4. Sum refers to counting up both Blends and Singles of *only* that specific determinant, while Sum All refers to counting up both Blends and Singles of all combinations of a Determinant; 5. Calculate a difference score between two entries and look up the Scaled Difference score on the D Score Conversion Table; 6. b; 7. Add C or $\boxed{23}$ under Singles and under Blends, $\boxed{17}$. Look for C's on the upper half of the Structural Summary form; 8. Total number of responses, or R, is calculated by counting the number of responses listed under the Resp. No. column on the Sequence of Scores sheet.

Five

PRINCIPLES OF INTERPRETATION

Nancy Kaser-Boyd and Susan Steinberg-Oren

Many students of psychology, not to mention practicing psychologists, are intimidated by the complex scoring system and interpretation guidelines of the Rorschach. The sheer number of Structural Summary variables, as well as their interrelationships, can be overwhelming to the new and briefly trained user. This chapter will provide examiners with an organized system showing how to group various score interpretations into meaningful hypotheses. This will be done in a step-by-step manner that explains Exner's Interpretive Search Strategy and places the variables, their means and standard deviations, and the interpretation of high and low scores in a clear, easy-to-access manner.

The interpretation process begins once the test information is scored properly and organized into the Structural Summary. This is a complex process that "includes a reasonably good knowledge of personality and behavioral theories, and expertise in psychopathology, and a knowledge of the test itself" (Exner, 1993, p. 321). The structural summary represents the database from which Rorschach interpretation springs.

Exner emphasizes that interpretation comes not from single scores, but from the *configuration* of scores. He also emphasizes that the interpretive process is one that begins with generating *hypotheses* about the examinee, which is a two-stage process. In the Propositional Stage, data from various interpretive clusters are analyzed. During this stage, the examinee's score should be compared to means and standard deviations for nonpatients and for relevant patient groups. Exner provides research data for a number of diagnostic groups in the tables of the third edition of Volume I of the *Comprehensive System* textbook (Exner, 1993). The examiner should be sensitive to the "fit" between the demographics of the reference sample and the examinee. In the Integration Stage, data from the clusters are combined and integrated into a meaningful description of the client. Exner (1993) states that integration is achieved not merely by adding hypotheses together "but . . . involves the clinical conceptualization of the psychology of a person (p. 325)." The interpretive process consists of a propositional stage and an integration stage (see Rapid Reference 5.1).

Exner created an interpretive cluster approach to the Rorschach as a way to organize the many scores and ratios on the Structural Summary. He subjected the Rorschach data to a formal cluster analysis that identified seven groups of intercorrelated variables, which he designated as Rorschach "clusters." Each is related to an aspect of personality functioning frequently examined by psychologists, for example, information processing, affect, self-perception, and the like. Table 5.1 lists these seven clusters and identifies the variables in each cluster as well as the means and standard deviations for the nonpatient sample. The seven clusters are: Information Processing, Cognitive Mediation, Ideation, Capacity for Control and Tolerance for Stress, Affect, Self-Perception, Interpersonal Perception and Relations (see Rapid Reference 5.2). In addition to these seven clusters, each structural summary should be examined for validity and for situational stress. Note that while the Suicide Constellation (S-Con) does not appear in any of the clusters, it is a crucial Rorschach variable that should be considered first, before the cluster analysis.

Theoretically these clusters can be examined in any order, but they are usually taken in an order suggested by the referral question or by Exner's Key Variables. What are Key Variables? Exner (1993) empirically identified Key Variables (see Weiner, 1998, p. 71) as those which yielded the most data for a particular record, that is, these were the most salient results for the subject and beginning here would be the most descriptive and parsimonious. To illustrate, if the examinee's record was positive on the Schizophrenia Index (SCZI), the most

Rapid Reference 5.1

Interpretive Process

Stage 1: Propositional Stage. Examinee's scores are compared to means and standard deviations for nonpatients and relevant patient groups. Hypotheses are generated.

Stage 2: Integration Stage. Data from clusters are combined and integrated into a meaningful description. Clinical conceptualization of the relevant personality variables of the person.

≡ Rapid Reference 5.2

Interpretive Clusters

Full Name	Shorthand Name
Information Processing	Processing
Cognitive Mediation	Mediation
Ideation	Ideation
Capacity for Control and Tolerance for Stress	Controls
Affect	Affect
Self-Perception	Self-Perception
Interpersonal Perception and Relations	Interpersonal Perception

productive order of examining clusters was Ideation, Mediation, Processing, Controls, Affect, Self-Perception, and finally, Interpersonal Perception. On the other hand, if the examinee's record yielded a DEPI > 5, the most productive order of variable analysis would be Affect, Controls, Self-Perception, Interpersonal Perception, Processing, Mediation, and Ideation. Examples of clusters ordered by referral question appear in Chapter 7 (a suicidal man and affect and a female stalker and her self-perception and interpersonal variables).

When the computer scoring program (RIAP) is used, the computer automatically searches for Key Variables and orders the clusters and interpretive hypotheses accordingly. This does not relieve the examiner from responsibility to know the basis of the interpretive statements generated by the computer.

PROFILE VALIDITY

Two variables are critical to profile validity: R and Lambda. R (number of responses) for adults is between 17 and 27 with a mean of 22.67 ($SD = 4.23$). If R is very low, the usefulness of most of the ratios and percentages is questionable. Exner suggests that records of less than 14 should be readministered (see Chapter 2 for administration instructions). Weiner (1998), however, emphasizes that there may still be some useful data in a short (i.e., R = 14 or less) protocol,

Table 5.1   Interpretive Clusters Exner, 1993

Means and Standard Deviations

Information Processing

L = 58 (.26)	W:D:Dd = 8.5:12.9:1.2
Zf = 11.8 (2.59)	W:M = 8.5:4.3
HVI Pos = 2%	OBS =
Zd = .72 (3.06)	DQ+ = 7.3 (2.16)
PSV = .05 (.22)	DQv/+ = .41 (.66)
	DQv = 1.3 (1.26)

Cognitive Mediation

Lamba = .58 (.26)	OBS =
P = 6.89 (1.38)	X+% = .79 (.08)
FQx+ = .90 (.92)	F+% = .71 (.17)
FQxo = 16.9 (3.34)	Xu% = .14 (.07)
FQxu = 3.25 (1.77)	X–% = .07 (.05)
FQx– = 1.44 (1.04)	S–% = .08 (.23)
FQxnone = .09 (.33)	CONFAB = .00 (.00)

Ideation

EB = 43:4.5	EBPer =
eb = 4.8:3.4	MOR = .70 (.82)
FM = 3.71 m = 1.12	2AB + Art + Ay = .20 (.09)
a:p = 6.48:2.69	MQual– = .03 (.18)
Ma:Mp = 3.03:1.31	MQualNone = .01 (.11)

Critical Special Scores

DV = .70 (.79)	DV2 = .01 (.10)
INC = .52 (.65)	INC2 = .00 (.07)
DR = .15 (.38)	DR2 = .00 (.04)
FAB = .17 (.41)	FAB2 = .02 (.13)
ALOG = .04 (.22)	
CON = .00 (.00)	Raw Sum6 = 1.59 (1.25)
SCZI = NEG	Wgtd Sum6 = 3.28 (2.89)

Table 5.1   continued

Capacity for Control and Tolerance for Stress

EB = 4.3:4.5	EA = 8.8 (2.18)
eb = 4.8:3.4	es = 8.2 (3.0)
FM = 3.71	C' = 1.53
T = 1.03	m = 1.12
V = .26	Y = 0.57
Adj D = .20 (.88)	PureC = .08 (.28)
Sum T = 1.03 (.58)	
Sum m = 1.12 (.85)	MQ– = .03 (.18)
Sum Y = .57 (1.0) MQnone = .01 (.11)	
D = .04 (1.09)	Adj D = .20 (.88)
Adj es = __	CDI = 4:3%

Situational Stress

D = .04	EA = 8.8
es = 8.2	Adj es = ~
ADJ D = .20	T = 1.03
m = 1.12	Y = .57
V = .26	Blends = 5.16 (1.93)
Color-shading Blends = .46 (.69)	

Affect

DEPI = >5:3%	EBPer = N/A
EB = 4.3:4.5	FC:CF+C = 4.09:1.88
eb = 4.8:3.4	Pure C = .08 (.28)
	SumC':WSumC = 1.53:4.5
C' = 1.53	Afr = .69 (.16)
T = 1.03	S = 1.47 (1.21)
V = .26	Blends/R = 5.16 (1.93)
Y = .57	CP = .02 (.14)

Table 5.1   continued

Self-Perception

3r + (2)/R = .39 (.07)	FD = 1.16 (.87)
Fr + rF = .08 (.35)	Sum V = .26 (.58)
MOR = .70 (.82)	Hx = .01 (.11)
An + Xy = .45	Sx = .07 (.39)
H: (H) + Hd + (Hd) = 3.39:2.0	

Interpersonal Perception and Relations

CDI = >4 = 3%	a:p = 6.48:2.69
T = 1.03	Human Cont =
Pure H = 3.39	HVI Pos = 2%
Food = .23 (.50)	PER = 1.05 (10)
COP = 2.07 (1.52)	AG = 1.18 (1.18)
Isolate/R = 0.45	

Responses to be read

Human Movement with Pair	Human Contents
(List and Examine)	(List and Examine)

particularly if the short protocol has extreme data (e.g., a number of M–responses or Morbids, a markedly low X+%, a high number of Space responses, etc.). Short records are found in examinees who are unusually defensive as well as those who are emotionally constricted or depressed or somewhat limited in cognitive abilities. Malingerers may also use the defensive strategy of giving few responses, simply because they are unsure how to "fake" mental illness.

Lambda is a second indicator of profile validity. Lambda is the proportion of pure F that has occurred in the record (number of Pure Form responses/number of non–Pure Form responses which is Total R minus Pure Form answers). Lambda generally falls between .59 and .94, and the mean in the non-patient population is .58 (*SD* = .026). Lambda > 1.2 signals a very simplistic response to the stimuli that ignores the complexity of the inkblots, and ignores color and shading. This may be due to extreme caution or defensiveness in responding, but is also seen in examinees who are emotionally constricted and

≡ Rapid Reference 5.3

Profile Validity

R (number of responses)		
	Range	17–27
	Mean	22.67
	SD	4.23
Lambda		
	Range	.59–.94
	Mean	.58
	SD	.026

who lack problem-solving resources. When Lambda is < .59, the examinee has included color or shading in many of their responses. Such a person may have difficulty responding to stimuli without the intrusion of emotion. There may be more affective responses than may be adaptive and the examinee may be overwhelmed by feelings. An analysis of Profile Validity is made by examining R and Lambda (see Rapid Reference 5.3).

S-CON

The Suicide Constellation was empirically derived by analyzing the Rorschach scores of patients who committed suicide within 60 days after taking the Rorschach. Exner compared this data to the Rorschachs of patients who attempted suicide, as well as to control groups of those who were depressed but not suicidal. The presence of some of these variables (see Rapid Reference 5.4) in the Suicide Constellation probably needs no explanation, but, briefly:

> *Vista* is found in people who are introspective and such people may be inclined to focus on their negative features.
> *Color Shading Blends* are found among people who have a mix of painful feelings. They may feel two or more ways about a person or an event, both of which are painful. Ambivalent, approach-avoidant, or conflicted are other ways to describe these individuals.
> *Egocentricity* <.31 is found in individuals who struggle with issues of self-worth.
> *Morbids* are obtained from percepts that are dead, damaged, or destroyed. The inkblots themselves do not call out morbid responses in

the typical subject, and the percept of something morbid is therefore a projection. These are empirically more common in depressed individuals or those with a highly pessimistic worldview. The Morbid score is also empirically associated with an impaired sense of self, that is, the "self" feels dead, damaged, destroyed.

Zd greater than 3.5 is found in individuals who make painstaking efforts to organize their worlds. They are called "overincorporators," and they may be obsessive or perfectionistic or make extraordinary efforts to make disparate perceptions "fit together," often at the expense of good reality-testing.

es greater than EA is found in individuals whose present experience of distress outweighs their capacity for coping.

X+% less than .70 is found in those whose reality testing is impaired. Typically this is because too much "projection" is occurring in the process of Rorschach responding and this projection is decreasing perceptual accuracy. In real-life situations, these individuals are susceptible to distorting reality. Misperception leads to behavior that is often quite inappropriate. Such a person might completely misperceive an interaction with another person, experiencing profound rejection or threat where there is none.

The CF + C greater than FC and S greater than 3 have to do with affect (emotion). At this level, they suggest a person who experences intense emotions, including anger, and these emotions may not be modulated by thought or other typical forms of emotional modulation.

A paragraph culled from the Suicide Constellation and the other affective variables might say: "The patient is experiencing intensely negative, probably very painful emotions. This creates a very disruptive impact on almost all emotional functioning. It tends to dominate the affective experiences of

≡ *Rapid Reference 5.4*

S-Con

1. FV + VF + V + FD > 2
2. Color-Shading Blends > 0
3. 3r + (2)/R < .31 or > .44
4. MOR > 3
5. Zd > +3.5 or Zd < −3.5
6. es > EA
7. CF + C > FC
8. X+% < .70
9. S > 3
10. P < 3 or P > 8
11. Pure H < 2
12. R < 17

the subject and can become a pervasive influence on thinking." The Suicide Constellation consists of 12 variables and is considered positive when 8 are present in a record (see Rapid Reference 5.4).

THE SEVEN CLUSTERS

The first three clusters fall into what Exner calls the Cognitive Triad, which includes Information Processing, Cognitive Mediation, and Ideation. Information Processing is conceptualized as the examinee's "input" of information from the stimuli. Mediation is the translation or identification of information that has been input. Ideation involves conceptualizing the information that has been translated. Some Rorschach variables appear in more than one cluster because they relate to more than one cluster and should be considered in analyzing the data from each cluster, which follows Exner's principle that Rorschach variables cannot be analyzed in isolation.

Information Processing

In the Information Processing cluster there are actually two subclusters, one that addresses the processing effort or motivation (Lambda, OBS, HVI, Zf, W:D:Dd, W:M), and one that provides information about the quality and efficiency of the processing (DQ, Zd, PSV, sequencing).

> *Processing effort.* Lambda was discussed earlier in this chapter under Profile Validity.
> *OBS.* When OBS is elevated, the examinee is prone to be perfectionistic. These individuals are often preoccupied with details, indecisive, and likely to have some difficulty expressing emotion. They are often over-incorporators (Zd > +3.0). This style can be adaptive in particular occupations, but it may cause the examinee to get "stuck" in details.
> *HVI.* If HVI is positive, the examinee may be hyperalert to environment. These individuals are guarded and often invest considerable energy to survey all the features of the stimulus field, which may result in superior processing, but it can also result in an unusual focus on particular aspects of the inkblots (e.g., a focus on their threatening quality). HVI was not positive in several groups who qualified for the diagnosis of Post-Traumatic Stress Disorder, possibly because their records contained at least one Texture response, or because their con-

striction rendered their records not rich enough to provide the necessary variables.

Zf indicates the frequency of organized responses. Most adults give about seven organized responses. A greater number can be due to higher intelligence or a greater need to account for the details of the world.

W:D:Dd. Exner calls this the Economy Index. If the ratio is weighted toward the W side in an average-length record, the examinee strives to excess in attempting to organize ambiguous stimuli. If weighted toward the D + Dd side, the examinee appears to select the easiest perceptual-cognitive "way out" when faced with ambiguity.

W:M. Exner calls this the Aspirational Ratio and describes it as an index of aspiration contrasted with capability. If W > M by more than three to one, aspirations likely exceed functioning level. If the ratio is less than two to one, aspirations are lower than the examinee is capable of striving for. DQ and Form Quality offer clarifying information about ability.

Processing Quality and Efficiency

DQ is a measure of "cognitive sophistication" or cognitive development. A greater number of DQ+ responses is typically associated with higher levels of cognitive functioning. If DQ+ is above average, the examiner might say, "The examinee tends to respond to his world by acknowledging and integrating disparate data, synthesizing or 'making sense of' data in a way that is consistent with good reality testing." When the examinee has a greater than average amount of DQv, his or her processing of input is likely to be vague and imprecise, and possibly impressionistic.

Zd is derived in the Table of Z (Zsum − Zest). If Zd is greater than +3, the examinee likely "overincorporates" or works very hard to weave everything together in his or her response. If Zd is greater than −3, the examinee is rather haphazard in his or her integration efforts and may strive for integration at a level that exceeds cognitive functioning.

PSV. The special score PSV is given when the examinee gives a second response with the exact same scores to the same card (Within-Card Perseveration) (Exner, 1993, p. 169) or repeats the same content (e.g, "Here is that bat again") across cards (Content Perseveration, Exner, 1993, p. 170). The perseveration response reflects cognitive inflexibility and

DON'T FORGET 5.1

Information Processing: Means and Standard Deviations

L = 58 (.26)

Zf = 11.8 (2.59)

HVI Pos = 2%

Zd = .72 (3.06)

PSV = .05 (.22)

DQv = 1.3 (1.26)

W:D:Dd = 8.5:12.9:1.2

W:M = 8.5:4.3

OBS is positive in 2% of nonpatients

DQ+ = 7.3 (2.16)

DQv/+ = .41 (.66)

in some cases a preoccupation with particular content. A third type, Mechanical Perseveration, Exner, 1993, p. 170, is uncommon and consists of giving essentially the same response over and over. This type is typically only seen in intellectually or neurologically impaired subjects.

Don't Forget 5.1 contains variables in the Information Processing Cluster.

Cognitive Mediation

This cluster examines how inputs are translated. In common-sense terms, the cluster looks at how stimuli are processed: Is reality testing good? Is the examinee relatively conventional? Is he idiosyncratic? Exner indicates that

DON'T FORGET 5.2

Cognitive Mediation: Means and Standard Deviation

Lamba = .58 (.26)

P = 6.89 (1.38)

FQx+ = .90 (.92)

FQxo = 16.9 (3.34)

FQxu = 3.25 (1.77)

FQx– = 1.44 (1.04)

FQxnone = .09 (.33)

OBS is positive in 2% of nonpatients

X+% = .79 (.08)

F+% = .71 (.17)

Xu% = .14 (.07)

X–% = .07 (.05)

S–% = .08 (.23)

CONFAB = .00 (.00)

Lambda and OBS (discussed earlier in this chapter) should be reviewed before interpreting any other data in the cluster, since these can have a substantial impact on mediation. With high Lambda, there is a tendency to oversimplify the stimulus field, which can lead to distortion and inaccuracy.

Populars. The average nonpatient gives between six and seven out of thirteen possible Popular responses. A large number of Populars can suggest a cautious, conventional approach to the test and possibly an overly conventional approach to the world. A low number of Populars may indicate that the examinee has difficulty seeing the world as others do, or possibly he or she rejects conventional approaches.

Form Quality. The Form Quality variable (FQx+, xo, xu, and x–) is a score that reflects the degree to which the examinee's response "fits" the basic form features of the inkblot. This fit is determined by referring to Table A in the workbook, a "frequency" table developed by examining hundreds of responses to the Rorschach inkblots, that provides information about common responses to the whole inkblots and frequently used parts of the inkblots. When we look at the nonpatient sample, of the approximately 22 responses, 17 were FQxo, 3 were FQxu, one was FQx+, and one FQx–. The FQx+ score reflects unusually detailed, elaborate responses that also fit the form features of the inkblot. When examinees give FQxu and FQx– responses, their "translation" of stimuli is unusual, if not idiosyncratic. FQx– responses reflect a complete failure of "fit" and therefore of reality testing. These scores are summarized in the F+%, X+%, Xu%, X–% and S–% scores described below.

F+% is the "accuracy" score for responses that only used Form. It is discussed as the Form Quality when the response did not "provoke emotion," and theoretically it should be higher than X+% since it reflects a simple and concrete approach to the inkblot. There are patient groups, however, who are not accurate when they give Pure Form responses, for example, schizophrenics, who may give a record that is largely form-based, but quite idiosyncratic.

X+% is the Form Quality for the entire record (pure Form and all other responses). This index is considered more reliable and meaningful than F+% because it is longer. The rare person has an X+% of 100. The cutting score is .70, and below this, reality testing is in question.

Xu% indicates the percentage of responses with "unusual" Form Quality. These responses are not "form failures" but involve "bending" reality somewhat and may be a result of projection or mildly idiosyncratic thinking. In the nonpatient sample, Xu% was 14 percent, so the average person does give responses that are not "ordinary" in Form Quality.

X–% indicates the percentage of "form failures" or completely arbitrary percepts. If this score is 15 percent or greater, the examinee has a significant tendency to distort reality.

S-% is the percentage of X– that contains S– responses (Sum SQ–/Sum FQx–). This score examines whether reality distortion is more marked when the examinee is responding to Space, that is, when the examinee experiences anger or the need to distance or exert autonomy.

CONFAB is scored when the examinee takes a detail of the inkblot and generalizes it to a larger area or the entire inkblot, inappropriate to the area, justifies this by referencing the small area first seen. Exner indicates that CONFAB is rare in most diagnostic conditions, and appears in this constellation because it represents an extreme form of cognitive dysfunction.

Don't Forget 5.2 contains variables in the Cognitive Mediation Cluster.

Ideation

The Ideation cluster provides data on how the translations of inputs become conceptualized and used. Exner states, "Ideation constitutes the core of psychological activity from which all decisions and deliberate behaviors evolve" (Exner, 1993, p. 473).

EB and EBPer. EB is a ratio comparing the sum of human movement responses to the weighted sum of color responses. Rorschach hypothesized that when the ratio is distinctly weighted in the M direction, the person is more prone to use his inner life for basic gratification and is considered "introversive." If EB is weighted on the color side of the ratio, the person is considered "extratensive" and is more prone to use the interactions between himself and his world for the gratification of basic needs. If both sides are relatively equal, the person is considered "ambitensive" and may be inconsistent in problem solving and decision making. Exner has done a great deal of work on the EB, which cannot be fairly summarized here. EBPer is a measure of preferred problem-solving style. It is calculated by dividing the larger number in the EB by the smaller number.

DON'T FORGET 5.3

Ideation: Means and Standard Deviation

EB = 43:4.5

eb = 4.8:3.4

FM = 3.71 m = 1.12

a:p = 6.48:2.69

Ma:Mp = 3.03:1.31

EBPer =

MOR = .70 (.82)

2AB + Art + Ay = .20 (.09)

MQual− = .03 (.18)

MQualNone = .01 (.11)

Critical Special Scores

DV = .70 (.79)

INC = .52 (.65)

DR = .15 (.38)

FAB = .17 (.41)

ALOG = .04 (.22)

CON = .00 (.00)

SCZI = NEG

DV2 = .01 (.10)

INC2 = .00 (.07)

DR2 = .00 (.04)

FAB2 = .02 (.13)

Raw Sum6 = 1.59 (1.25)

Wgtd Sum6 = 3.28 (2.89)

Eb. This ratio compares nonhuman movement to shading and achromatic color determinants. It provides information concerning stimulus demands, and when stimulus demands are examined in this index, the focus is on the left side of the index (FM+m). Exner indicates that if these scores are elevated above average, deliberate and focused ideational activity will be interrupted, impairing attention and concentration. When the right side of this ratio is high, the person is experiencing painful internalized affect.

a:p. A measure of the cognitive flexibility of the examinee. If the a:p ratio is heavily weighted to one side, the ideational set and values of the examinee are well fixed and may be difficult to alter.

Ma:Mp. The interpretation of this ratio is similar to that for a:p, except that Exner has conducted research with M and fantasy. He indicates that when Mp is at least one point higher than Ma, examinees have a stylistic tendency to use fantasy excessively. They are prone to defensively substitute fantasy for reality in stressful situations much more often than most people. If the value for Mp is two or more points greater than Ma, there is a marked style in which a flight into fantasy has become a routine tactic for dealing with unpleasant situations. They may deny reality and be avoidant and dependant in their orientation to problem solving.

M– is scored when there is poor Form Quality in a response in which there is human movement. When M– occurs in the record, conceptualizations about human interaction are likely to be unrealistic and may be marked by projection. Exner (1993) has said that even one M– is sufficient to raise concern about peculiarity in ideation. Two M– responses is unusual and if more than two occur, the presence of disoriented, strange thinking is practically certain. The examinee can also obtain an M– score by giving abstract and symbolic responses such as "it looks like depression." This is probably more obviously a serious failure of logical thinking.

There is probably more research on M than on most Rorschach variables. Numerous studies have found a positive correlation between M and IQ. Research demonstrates the development of M as children progress through developmental stages and a decline of M in the elderly. M is more common in individuals who are manic and less common in those who are depressed. M– occurred in 6 out of 200 nonpsychiatric records, 18 out of 100 outpatients, and 48 out of 125 schizophrenic records.

Intellectualization Index. This index includes the contents Abstract, Art, and Anatomy (2AB+Art+Ay). When these scores appear in the record, they are empirically related to the use of the defensive process of intellectualization. Individuals with elevated scores on this index tend to deny the presence of affect, reducing the likelihood that feelings will be dealt with directly or realistically. This approach becomes less effective as the magnitude of affective stimuli increases.

Morbids and Other Special Scores. The Morbid score has been studied frequently in the records of depressed subjects, and is part of S-Con and DEPI. When Morbid is scored, the examinee has seen an object as dead, damaged, or destroyed, or given a distinctly dysphoric quality to his or her response. Exner indicates that when MOR > 3, it is very likely that the thinking of the examinee is marked by a pessimistic set in which relationships are viewed with a sense of doubt or discouragement and gloomy outcomes are anticipated.

Regarding the other Special Scores, we will focus on the Raw Sum 6 and Wsum6 rather than each individual Special Score, except to say that the Special Scores reflect the way or ways in which the examinee distorts reality. The way the examinee's logical thinking goes awry is often illustrated by the types of Special Scores they have. This chapter will not attempt to provide interpretive statements for each Special Score; the reader is referred to Exner (1993) and Weiner (1998) for comprehensive discussions of the Special Scores. Exner indicates that many records will contain at least one of the critical Special Scores, especially the scores that are less serious forms of cognitive slippage. In the nonpatient sample, there was a mean of 4 for WSum6. He suggests using a cutting score of two standard deviations above the mean, as well as looking at the type of Special Score obtained (e.g., ALOGs versus DRs, level 2s versus level 1s).

Don't Forget 5.3 includes variables in the Ideation Cluster.

Capacity for Control and Tolerance for Stress

This constellation includes the set of variables Exner calls the Foursquare, about which he has conducted considerable study, ultimately evolving a method of evaluating current stress compared to the examinee's typical experience of stress. To the Rorschach newcomer, this set of variables can be confusing, and summarizing the research that led to the development of these variables is beyond the scope of this chapter. Here, we provide a simple overview of the basic variables in this constellation and how to use them to evaluate current levels of stress and the examinee's ability to cope with them.

Table 5.2   The Foursquare

EB	EA	D
eb	es	Adjusted D

To understand the Foursquare, it is easiest conceptually to start with Exner's work with the variables m and Y. In analog research, Viglione (1980) found it was relatively easy to elevate m and Y by experimentally inducing anxiety. A real-world study with Israeli navy men found m and Y to elevate during sea maneuvers. Of the variables in the eb, m and Y have the least temporal stability, seemingly because they respond to temporary or situational conditions. Because of this research, Exner developed a statistical method to account for the current or situationally based stress that the examinee may be experiencing. This method involves subtracting all but one m

DON'T FORGET 5.4

Capacity for Control and Tolerance for Stress: Means and Standard Deviations

EB = 4.3:4.5   EA = 8.8 (2.18)
eb = 4.8:3.4   es = 8.2 (3.0)
FM = 3.71   C' = 1.53
T = 1.03   m = 1.12
V = .26   Y = 0.57
Adj D = .20 (.88)   PureC = .08 (.28)
Sum T = 1.03 (.58)
Sum m = 1.12 (.85)   MQ– = .03 (.18)
Sum Y = .57 (1.0) MQnone = .01 (.11)
D = .04 (1.09)
Adj D = .20 (.88)   CDI > 4 in 3% of
                                               nonpatients

Situational Stress: Means and Standard Deviations
D = .04   EA = 8.8
es = 8.2   Adj es = ~
ADJ D = .20   T = 1.03
m = 1.12   Y = .57
V = .26   Blends = 5.16 (1.93)
Color-shading Blends = .46 (.69)

and one Y from the eb ratio. Other portions of the Foursquare, for example, the left side of EB and EA, contain scores that have been empirically related to coping capacities. It is obvious that the left side of the EB reflects coping ability, since it is a measure of ideation and is related to intelligence and creativity. EA is the sum of Movement and weighted color responses in the record and, as such, reflects the intellectual and emotional resources that the individual brings to bear on a problem. The M side reflects thinking and contemplating and the WSumC side reflects expressing emotion. Weiner (1998, p. 139) states, "The nature of M-type and WsumC-type activities makes the sum of M and WsumC a useful index of how many resources people have available for planning and implementing deliberate strategies of coping, with decision-making and problem-solving situations. . . . The more EA subjects have in their record, the more adaptive capacity they have at their disposal and the more competence they are likely to display in pursuing their aims and objectives" (p. 139). A minimally adequate amount of M:WSumC is 2:2.5, and a minimally adequate EA is 6. Examinees with an EA less than 6 could be described as having limited coping resources to meet life's demands.

The next part of the Foursquare is eb, the "experience base," which is composed of FM + m:Sum of all Shading. FM is said to measure the "disconcerting awareness of needs that are not being met" (Weiner, 1993, p. 123). The m score is said to indicate the feeling of being controlled by external forces or being helpless to prevent people or events from creating outcomes. Weiner summarizes the left side of the experience base (FM + m) as "ideation which is occurring when people would prefer to stop thinking about whatever is on their mind and think about some other topic instead, but find themselves unable to do so" (p. 123).

The right side of eb is the sum of all the shading responses. These include C', T, V, and Y. When we examine interpretive statements for these variables, we will see that they all reflect what Exner calls "painful internal states." It is no surprise that when the left and right sides of the "experience base" are summed, to become es or "experienced stimulation," they reflect internal needs and feelings that are pressing on the examinee.

The D and Adjusted D (Adj D) score in this variable cluster are calculated by subtracting es from EA and entering Table 10 in the Rorschach workbook. D and Adj D are standard scores. Adj D is derived after adjusting for current stress, the mechanism discussed at the beginning of this section. All but one Y and one m are subtracted from es and then EA–es is recomputed, Table 10 is entered again, thus yielding Adj D. Weiner (1998) points out that D derives from conjoint consideration of almost all of the determinants coded in the Comprehensive System and as a result is one of the most broadly based, dependable, and interpretively meaningful summary scores. Suggested cutting scores and their interpretive significance are:

D = 0, the normal range. Such a person is described as free from overt anxiety, tension, nervousness, and irritability. They have average capacities to tolerate frustration and to persevere in stressful situations.

D+. Individuals who are D+ have a good amount of coping ability and resources in reserve. They have good stress tolerance. Negative aspects of the D+ (i.e., having difficulty understanding people who are easily overwhelmed) are possible and should be evaluated in conjunction with other test data.

D–. These individuals likely feel tense and irritable, have a limited tolerance for frustration, and a tendency to be impulsive. The D– person, according to Weiner (1998) is susceptible to "unwelcome, unpleasant, and episodic losses of self-control" (p. 145).

The D score reflects the amount of stress experienced at the time of test administration, and Adj D reflects how the examinee might be if current stressors were "subtracted" from the record. To illustrate, suppose the examinee had an EA of 5 and an es of 15. EA–es equals –10 and the D score is –3, which reflects a person in crisis whose stress outstrips current coping abilities. Suppose further that the examinee has 3 m and 4 Y. Computing Adj D would result in subtracting 5 from es; EA–es then becomes –5 and Adj D would be –1.

The two remaining variables in this cluster are MQ– and CDI. It is fairly easy to see why Human Movement with minus form quality would appear in this constellation—simply put, if the ability to generate M responses is a reflection of intellectual resources and problem-solving capacity, when the M is a minus Form Quality, this capacity is seriously awry. CDI is an empirically derived set of variables that includes some of the above scores (e.g., EA and Adj D) but adds new ones as well (e.g., Texture) to survey difficulties coping adequately with stress, affect, and interpersonal relationships. See Exner's volume I (1993) for a discussion of the creation of CDI. A CDI greater than 4 is required and signifies a deficit in coping abilities. Weiner (1998) emphasizes the need to look at CDI along with EA, indicating that an elevated CDI with low EA identifies a deficit in adaptive skills, whereas an elevated CDI with higher EA indicates pockets of deficit, most likely surrounding interpersonal relationships (i.e., the other variables in the index).

Don't Forget 5.4 includes variables in the Capacity for Control Cluster.

Affect

Reviewing the examinee's affect begins with an examination of S-Con, as noted above. The next important variable, a "Key variable" in Exner's ver-

> # DON'T FORGET 5.5
>
> ## Affect: Means and Standard Deviations
>
> | | |
> |---|---|
> | DEPI > 5 in 3% of nonpatients | EBPer = N/A |
> | EB = 4.3:4.5 | FC:CF+C = 4.09:1.88 |
> | eb = 4.8:3.4 | Pure C = .08 (.28) |
> | | SumC':WSumC = 1.53:4.5 |
> | c' = 1.53 | Afr = .69 (.16) |
> | T = 1.03 | S = 1.47 (1.21) |
> | V = .26 | Blends/R = 5.16 (1.93) |
> | Y = .57 | CP = .02 (.14) |

nacular, is the Depression Index (DEPI). DEPI was empirically derived and is considered positive if five or more conditions are true (Exner, 1993). A number of the variables in DEPI surround affect. The exceptions are one variable that is related to interpersonal adjustment (COP) and one related to the self-perception cluster (Egocentricity/Reflections). When the examinee is positive on DEPI, the interpretive statement is "the subject has many of the features that are common among those diagnosed as being depressed or having an affective disorder. . . . It may also indicate that the psychological organization of the subject can easily give rise to depression or fluctuations in mood" (Exner, 1993, p. 360).

Afr provides an index of the extent to which the examinee is affected by the color cards. If Afr < .55, the examinee is withdrawing from affective stimuli, possibly to avoid loss of control over affect. If Afr > .75, the examinee may tend to get "caught up in" affective stimuli.

EB and eb are included in this cluster as a measure of the preferred coping style of the individual (i.e., introversive or extratensive) and the press of internal needs on the examinee. The previous cluster discussed these variables in detail.

Blends are examined to determine whether feelings too often merge with thinking in problem solving. The typical nonpatient has five Blends in his or her record. A larger number (generally, two standard deviations from the mean) is seen in individuals who too often mix feelings with thinking, and whose thinking may be overly complex.

Color-Shading Blends. Feelings may mix in a particularly painful way in individuals with Color-Shading Blends. They may be rather explosive and not controlled by logic if there is Pure C in the record. If CF + C > FC, the same may be said: emotions can be unmodulated and intense at times. *C', V, T, and Y* reflect dysphoric emotions (depression, painful self-examination, need for closeness, and anxiety). C' is scored when the subject has used black, white, or grey in forming his or her response. It is empirically tied to dysphoric affect and internalized tension. Early research with C' found that alcoholics gave more of this score (Weber, 1937, in Exner, volume I, 1993). In Exner's research, 78% of the group that was clinically depressed gave at least one C' and the mean was 2.16 compared to 1.53 for nonpatients, 1.05 for schizophrenics, and .83 for the character-disordered group. Inpatient depressives who are retested at discharge, when they are less depressed, usually give fewer than half the number of C' responses even though the retest records are longer. Exner (1993, p. 387) states that Vista is found in individuals who are "involved in ruminative self-inspection focused on perceived negative features of the self." Vista (V) occurs in only 20% of the adult nonpatient normative sample. It, too, occurs more frequently in the records of seriously depressed patients: 56% of the depressed inpatient sample had one Vista, and Vista was much more frequent in the records of those who attempted suicide. Vista has been found to increase in patients involved in uncovering forms of therapy.

Texture (T) was postulated by Klopfer to be related to affection and dependency. Empirical studies have found a relationship between T and emotional need. For example, Exner and Bryant (1974) found that recently divorced or separated subjects had significantly more T than matched controls (3.57 compared to 1.31). T was found to increase after 9 to 15 months of treatment, regardless of its type. Certain groups were found more likely to have "T-less records," including battered women and children in foster care. Exner discussed these as individuals who may have "given up" hope of a close, affectionate relationship. If the record has a greater than average amount of T, the examinee may have a greater need for closeness or experience loneliness or stronger than usual dependency needs. People with no T appear to be more guarded or distant in interpersonal contact and more concerned about issues of personal space.

Y is scored when the subject uses diffuse shading. There is a significant degree of research on this variable that is summarized in Exner (1993, beginning at p. 391). Y is empirically tied to the experience of anxiety, and it has been shown to be present in people rated as significantly anxious by their therapists, and also to be affected by experimentally induced anxiety. Exner considers it very sensitive to stress, and it is an important part of the D score and the Adjusted D.

The S score, when two standard deviations above the mean for nonpatients (or $S \geq 4$), suggests a tendency to be oppositional and possibly have fairly longstanding feelings of anger or resentment.

CP (Color Projection) is a relatively rare score, to be given when the examinee sees a percept in color in response to a black-and-white (i.e., achromatic) inkblot. This reflects a form of denial, usually denial of dysphoric affect.

Don't Forget 5.5 includes variables in the Affect Cluster.

Self-Perception

This cluster contains some variables that seem overtly related to self-perception, that is, Egocentricity, as well as variables that seem more peripheral, such as Whole H: Part H.

3r + (2)/R is called the Egocentricity Index. If it is less than .39, there is low self-valuation, perhaps created by excessive concern for the values of the external world. If it is greater than .40, there may be excessive value

---

DON'T FORGET 5.6

Self-Perception: Means and Standard Deviations

3r + (2)/R = .39 (.07)	FD = 1.16 (.87)
Fr + rF = .08 (.35)	Sum V = .26 (.58)
MOR = .70 (.82)	Hx = .01 (.11)
An + Xy = .45	Sx = .07 (.39)
H: (H) + Hd + (Hd) = 3.39:2.0	

on the self, or excessive self-focus, which is not necessarily positive self-focus. Individuals who are depressed can be elevated here, and in that case, there is often a good deal of focus on perceived negative qualities.
Fr + rF. Reflections are more common in the records of children (e.g., 32% of the records of five year olds, 8% of the records of 11 year olds, 14% at age 14) but usually disappear during adolescence (Exner, volume 1, 3rd ed., p. 432). Reflections occur in roughly 7% of the adult nonpatient sample but are more common in the records of patients. Exner (1993) reports that Reflections are present in 10% of the records of depressed patients and 13% of the schizophrenia sample (p. 433). Like the data of Gacano and Meloy (1994), Exner's character-disordered sample has the greatest number of Reflections, about 20%, a finding that has been replicated in the research with male stalkers and sexually aggressive psychopaths. Gacano, Meloy, and Berg (1992) found that 50% of psychopaths have at least one Reflection response, and of the groups of men diagnosed Narcissistic and Borderline, 50% and 33% of the records contain at least one Reflection. Berg, Gacano, Meloy, and Peaslee (1994) looked at women diagnosed Borderline and found that only 28% of the records contained a Reflection response. The earliest research on the Reflection score was analog. Jones (1965) explored the relationship between the use of personal pronouns on the Sentence Completion Blank and the occurrence of Reflections on the Rorschach. Eighty subjects from a larger sample were selected, 40 with the highest number of "I" statements (high S) and 40 with the lowest number (low S). Reflection responses appeared in the records of 37 of the 40 subjects from the "high S" group.

As with other variables discussed in this chapter, as a general rule scores on this variable are interpretable if they are two standard deviations from the mean for nonpatients. Since most nonpatient records contain no Reflections, the presence of two Reflection responses is significant and suggests excessive self-focus.

FD. This variable is empirically related to self-examination. Studies of patients in psychotherapy found an increase in FD (Exner, 1993, Volume I). *V* (Vista) is also related to self-examination. When V > 0, the examinee likely has self-critical attitudes that become increasingly negative as V grows larger. Weiner (1998) states, "The more V in a record, the more likely it is that subjects' attitudes toward some aspects of themselves or their actions have progressed from displeasure and dissatisfaction to disgust and loathing" (p. 157).

MOR is found in the records of depressed and pessimistic individuals, which is not surprising given that this score is given for a percept of dead, damaged, diseased objects. Records in which MOR > 2 are very infrequent. Empirically these individuals tend to engage in a significant degree of negative self-evaluation. An elevation on MOR reflects highly negative feelings about the self, often about one's body, and vulnerability to damage is also often conveyed.

Hx. This variable is scored when the examinee gives a human emotion as his or her response to the inkblot, for example, "It just looks like depression" or "It looks like hate." Since the inkblots clearly do not call for specific emotional content, it should be obvious that these responses reflect projected aspects of the examinee's feelings about him- or herself or the world.

An + Xy. This content variable often reflects an unusual concern with body integrity. The actual content provides further data for interpretation, but these should be regarded as hypotheses and used cautiously.

Sx. Sex responses are quite uncommon on the Rorschach even though there are some portions of the inkblots that clearly "pull" for sex responses. In the nonpatient sample, most records didn't have even one sex response. When a sex response does occur it provides hypotheses about sexual experience and sexual interactions. For example, sex responses are more frequent in populations of women who have been subjected to repeated violent marital sex (Kaser-Boyd, 1999).

H:Hd + (H) + (Hd). This ratio explores differences in Whole Human percepts and Part-Human or fantasied human percepts. This ratio could also be examined in the Interpersonal Perception cluster. In both domains (i.e., self and other), if the ratio is weighted to the right side, the examinee tends to have unrealistic or fantasied expectations of human interactions. If the ratio is weighed to the left side, perceptions of self and others tend to be realistic and others are experienced as whole beings rather than as fragmented parts.

Don't Forget 5.6 includes variables in the Self-Perception Cluster.

Interpersonal Perception and Relations

CDI has three variables that concern interaction: AG and COP and Texture. The tendency to see human interaction as inherently cooperative or aggressive and the need for or dependency on relationships is related to coping and problem-solving ability. Each of these "interpersonal" variables is discussed in this chapter.

HVI. The crucial variable in HVI is T, that is, T must be absent for HVI to be positive. Individuals who are "hypervigilant" upon clinical examinations may be negative on HVI because they have T in their record. Some clinically "hypervigilant" patients have more of an "approach-avoidance" conflict toward others—they are needy and want to be close, but they fear abuse or rejection. Other variables in HVI tap preoccupation with human interaction [H + (H) + Hd + (Hd)]; a high proportion fantasied content, tendency to see part-human rather than whole figures, and seeing figures with protective garb (Cg > 3).

a:p. If this ratio is significantly weighted to one side, the examinee ap-

DON'T FORGET 5.7

Interpersonal Perception and Relations: Means and Standard Deviations

CDI > 4 in 3% of nonpatients

T = 1.03

Pure H = 3.39

Food = .23 (.50)

COP = 2.07 (1.52)

Isolate/R = 0.45

a:p = 6.48:2.69

Human Cont =

HVI Pos = 2% of nonpatients

PER = 1.05 (10)

AG = 1.18 (1.18)

Responses to be read

Human Movement with Pair

(List and Examine)

Human Contents

(List and Examine)

pears to have a preference in interaction and problem-solving style, e.g., passive or active. If the ratio is approximately equal, they are said to have an uncertain interaction or problem-solving style, and the lack of consistency may cause problems, especially if they are uncertain about which approach to use.

Pure H is interpreted the same way in this constellation as in the Self-Perception cluster.

Food. Although food seems like it might be a common response to Rorschach inkblots, in the nonpatient sample, there was only one Food response for every four records. Food responses have been empirically associated with a focus on need-satisfaction.

T. See the discussion of Texture under Affect, (page 131).

COP. When present, the examinee likely sees human interaction as having the potential for mutually cooperative behavior.

AG. When present, the examinee likely sees human interaction as having the potential for aggressive and threatening behavior.

Isolate/R. If this ratio is more than one quarter of the record, there is a significant likelihood of social withdrawal and interpersonal isolation.

PER. While Personalization (PER) is usually thought of as a measure of defensiveness, in this constellation, it becomes important to look at the verbalization in the PER. Is it self-justifying? Is it self-aggrandizing and proud? Sometimes the PER is simply an attempt by the examinee to tell the examiner about him- or herself. The specific type of PER will add information about the examinee's interactive style. Don't Forget 5.7 includes variables in the Interpersonal Perception Cluster.

INTEGRATION

When the examiner has worked his or her way through the validity indicators, S-Con, and the seven clusters, he or she will have a set of hypotheses, organized into meaningful "chunks" that relate to cognitive, emotional, and interpersonal variables. The Rorschach provides very detailed information about the seven areas of psychological functioning identified by the clusters. The examiner must be cautious when relating Rorschach data to diagnostic cate-

DON'T FORGET 5.8

Basic Interpretive Guidelines

The profile should be examined for validity before interpretation proceeds, since high Lambda records can significantly reduce many of the scores, ratios, and constellations.

Use means and standard deviations for relevant reference groups to determine cutting scores for interpretive significance.

The statements generated from the Rorschach interpretive strategy are *hypotheses*, to be integrated with data from other tests, interview, and life-history data.

gories. More often than not, the hypotheses relate only indirectly to the Diagnostic and Statistical Manual (DSM-IV) classifications. The next step is Integration, and this involves discarding hypotheses that are in conflict or do not seem well founded when the history of the examinee is considered. The final step is an integration of Rorschach data with data from the Mental Status Examination, clinical interview, life history, collateral sources, and other psychological tests. Chapters 7 and 8 illustrate this process. Don't Forget box 5.8 reviews basic interpretive guidelines.

🖎 TEST YOURSELF 🖎

1. **The Intellectualization Index is a measure of how intelligent the examinee is.** True or False?

2. **A "Key Variable" is a Rorschach variable that**
   (a) is critical in every Rorschach record.
   (b) yields the most data for a particular Rorschach record.
   (c) shouldn't be ignored.
   (d) all of the above.

3. **If interpretive hypotheses from one cluster conflict with those from another cluster, the examiner should**
   (a) choose the hypothesis that comes first in the interpretive search strategy.
   (b) choose the hypothesis that makes the most "common sense."
   (c) choose the hypothesis that seems supported by the clinical history and presentation.
   (d) none of the above.

4. S-Con is examined before the search through the seven clusters because

(a) S-Con isn't included in the interpretive search clusters.

(b) Suicide potential is critical to case management and takes precedence over other aspects of personality description.

(c) S-Con can modify the interpretation of other clusters.

(d) b & c.

5. Data generated during the proposition and integration states of Rorschach interpretation are ultimately integrated with

(a) Mental Status Examination.

(b) life history.

(c) observable or reported symptoms.

(d) data from other psychological tests or measures.

(e) all of the above.

Answers: 1. False; 2. b; 3. c; 4. d; 5. e.

Six

STRENGTHS AND WEAKNESSES OF THE RORSCHACH

Nancy Kaser-Boyd, Ph.D.

OVERVIEW OF ADVANTAGES AND DISADVANTAGES OF THE RORSCHACH

The Rorschach has been the subject of discussion and controversy for many years, with strident attackers and defenders. Why one test instrument so inflames controversy is somewhat puzzling. Possibly it comes from the fact that the Rorschach is so unique as a psychological measure, or possibly its early users were too grandiose in their claims about the Rorschach. The Exner Comprehensive System has standardized the administration and scoring of the Rorschach, and tied interpretation to empirical data. This means that the Rorschach of today is a somewhat different method than that of Klopfer's days or even the Rorschach methods of the early 1980s. This chapter reviews some of the strengths and weaknesses of the Rorschach method.

≡ Rapid Reference 6.1

Strengths and Weaknesses of Rorschach Development

Strengths

- Developed historically from a variety of perspectives including perception and learning, experimental psychology, and psychoanalytic theory.

- Exner Comprehensive System developed empirically by studying the logic and experimental soundness of variables generated by five different scoring systems.

Weaknesses

- Not originally developed for the purpose to which it is now put.

- At least five different scoring systems developed, which resulted in five different Rorschachs and created confusion with Rorschach research.

≡ Rapid Reference 6.2

Strengths and Weaknesses of Standardization and Norms

Strengths

- Administration is standardized with the Exner Comprehensive System.

- Scoring the Rorschach has been standardized with the Exner Comprehensive System, based on Exner's empirical analysis of the suggested scores of Beck, Klopfer, Hertz, Pietrovski.

- There is a large normative sample with detailed descriptive statistics for adults and children, including 700 nonpatient adults and 1,390 children aged 5 to 16.

- Normative data concerning the Rorschach scores and constellations are available and allow a comparison of individuals to appropriate reference groups. For example, Exner provides data on 320 hospitalized schizophrenics, 315 hospitalized depressives, 440 outpatients, and 180 outpatients with character disorders. Weiner (1998) notes this is more standardization information than is available for most psychological assessment measures.

- Cross-validation research provides reference samples for other diagnostic groups, for example, see Lerner and Lerner (1980) on BPD, Gacano and Meloy (1994) on ASPD, Kaser-Boyd (1993) on victims of domestic violence, Nash (1993) on women with childhood sexual abuse.

Weaknesses

- Even with standardized scoring instructions, inter-rater reliability is between .85 and .90.

- There is a lack of research with minority populations, but see Krall (1983) for norms for Black inner-children; Reichlin (1984) for older Americans; DeVoss and Boyer (1989) on Japanese-Americans, and Sachs and Lee (1992) on Chinese in Hong Kong.

≡ Rapid Reference 6.3

Strengths and Weaknesses on Reliability of the Rorschach

Strengths

- Studies of inter-rater reliability typically show levels of agreement of about 90% for location scores, pairs, populars, and Z scores. For Form Quality, Special Scores, and Content, the reliability coefficients are in the mid-80s.

- Test-retest data/studies in adults show stability coefficients of .80 or more for many Rorschach variables.

Weaknesses

- Inter-rater reliability may be low in Rorschach examiners who are not well trained or experienced.

- Test-retest correlations are lower in conditions where examinees can be expected to change, for example, children progressing through developmental stages, patients with mood disorders or a fluctuating psychotic disorder.

CAUTION 6.1

Abilities Not Measured Well by the Rorschach

- I.Q.
- Memory
- Neuropsychological impairment
- Learning disabilities
- Daily living skills
- Violence potential

≡ Rapid Reference 6.4

Strengths and Weaknesses of Validity of the Rorschach

Strengths

- Clinical utility. Surveys of clinical settings such as Piotrowski and Keller's (1989) of 413 outpatient mental health facilities, found that more than 80% of the responding agencies used the Rorschach. Watkins, Campbell, Nieberding, and Hallmark (1995) surveyed 412 clinical psychologists engaged in providing assessment services and 82% indicated they use the Rorschach in their assessments. The only methods mentioned by a greater percentage were the clinical interview (95%), the WAIS (93%), the MMPI (85%), and the Sentence Completion (84%).

- The Rorschach, administered and scored with the Exner Comprehensive System, is now the most accepted system in America and Western Europe and is the system most taught in American graduate schools.

- Because it is an ambiguous, unstructured task, the Rorschach produces data that may not be produced by self-report measures.

- The Rorschach has been very widely studied. Butcher and Rouse (1966) found the Rorschach was second to the MMPI in research articles published from 1974 to 1994. The Rorschach had an annual 20-year mean of 95.8 articles.

Weaknesses

- Much of the criticism of the Rorschach results from research conducted before the wide use of the Exner Comprehensive System.

- The Rorschach has differential clinical validity depending on the number of responses and the Lambda score. Some protocols are so brief that they do not yield much useful data.

- Though meta-analytic findings demonstrate at least some and perhaps substantial validity for the Rorschach, they do not constitute proof that every facet of the Rorschach has known and valid correlates (Weiner, 1996).

≡ Rapid Reference 6.4 (continued)

Strengths and Weaknesses of Validity of the Rorschach

Strengths

- Meta-analytic studies (e.g., Parker, Hanson, & Hunsley, 1988) found validity coefficients for the Rorschach not significantly different than those for the MMPI (.46 and .41, which were deemed adequate). They concluded that the MMPI and Rorschach have acceptable and roughly equivalent psychometric properties when used in appropriate circumstances.

Weaknesses

- Validity studies indicate validity only for the purpose indicated.

≡ Rapid Reference 6.5

Strengths and Weaknesses of Administration and Scoring

Strengths

- Administration procedures are simple and standardized.

- Administration procedures are the same for adults and children, with minor changes in administration procedures for ADHD children.

- Scoring rules are standardized.

Weaknesses

- The difficult examinee can be a challenge to test, especially for the inexperienced examiner.

- The administration must be done by an examiner who is also sophisticated in scoring, otherwise the inquiry may be inadequate for scoring purposes.

- Because there are an infinite number of percepts, scoring rules may sometimes need to be interpreted for the complex, unusual response.

≡ Rapid Reference 6.6

Strengths and Weaknesses of Interpretation

Strengths

- The Rorschach is a multifaceted method that provides a wealth of data about cognitive and emotional variables that can be analyzed quantitatively and qualitatively and interpreted from different theoretical perspectives.

- Rorschach interpretation with the Exner Comprehensive System has been empirically driven and there are numerous research studies on which to base interpretations of scores, constellations, and indices.

- Rorschach data can be integrated with data from other psychological tests because interpretive correlates are written in the language of general psychological descriptions of cognitive and emotional variables.

Weaknesses

- Competent interpretation of the Rorschach requires advanced training.

- Interpretation involves prioritizing variables based on referral questions and the interpretive search strategies and therefore requires the examiner to weigh various factors.

- Interpretation requires a working knowledge of personality structure and dynamics and psychopathology.

- Interpretation is the least well-taught subject in basic Rorschach training.

- Interpretation requires the examiner to become knowledgeable about Rorschach research, especially for the population he or she is testing.

 TEST YOURSELF

1. **It is more difficult to correctly administer the Rorschach for an examiner who doesn't know how to score the Rorschach because**

   (a) the Inquiry is designed primarily to elicit details that will be used in coding, especially determinants.

   (b) the examiner will passively take what the subject says and be unaware of what is missing.

   (c) the examiner is more likely to feel insecure with a real subject.

   (d) all of the above.

2. **The critics of the Rorschach's reliability are inaccurate when they cite**

   (a) poor test-retest reliability in children.

   (b) poor test-retest reliability in patients with fluctuating mood states.

   (c) poor test-retest reliability in examinees taking the test over short periods of time (i.e., 2 months).

   (d) a and b.

3. **The question "Is the Rorschach a valid test?" should really be "For what purposes has the Rorschach Inkblot Method been validated?"** True or False?

4. **Validation research on the Rorschach can be found**

   (a) in Exner's three volumes.

   (b) in several different texts on the Rorschach.

   (c) in journals such as the *Journal of Personality Assessment* and *Psychological Assessment*.

   (d) all of the above.

5. **The Rorschach has reference groups against which to compare the examinee that include which clinical groups?**

Answers: 1. a; 2. d; 3. True; 4. d; 5. adult nonpatients, schizophrenics, inpatient depressives, outpatient depressives, character disorders.

Seven

CLINICAL APPLICATIONS OF THE RORSCHACH

Nancy Kaser-Boyd, Ph.D.

There are many scores or configurations of scores on a Rorschach Structural Summary. Exner (1993) describes the Rorschach as a cognitive-perceptual task and, as such, it yields data about cognitive/ intellectual aspects of functioning such as perception, problem solving, and cognitive "style," and aspects of functioning that are more emotional, such as affect modulation, worldview, and self- and other representations. It becomes burdensome and can be confusing to systematically address every possible variable that can be derived from a Rorschach, and a good assessment sticks to the referral questions and is parsimonious. Because the Rorschach is time-consuming to administer and score, it is typically selected because of its ability to assess certain aspects of psychological functioning.

The Rorschach is very good at capturing the experiences and worldview or self- and object-representations of the examinee. To illustrate, two examinees may have identical elevations on the MMPI-2 — elevated scales 2, 4, and 8, but if examinee one's Rorschach is dominated by Morbids and threatening content, and Examinee two's record has Aggressive content and two Reflections, the dynamics of their 2-4-8 profiles are considerably different. Examinee one is quite likely a person with affects of depression and anxiety who sees the world as a threatening place. These scores are commonly found in individuals who have been through trauma or victim experiences. Examinee two's protocol is more consistent with the Rorschach scores found in personality disorders with pathological self-focus and an aggressive stance toward others.

The Rorschach also provides a very good sample of an examinee's perceptual accuracy and reality testing. The individual examinee may present quite well in the clinical setting, especially if aware of social convention, but the abstract stimuli of the Rorschach often "pull" for idiosyncratic content

CAUTION 7.1

Tips for Using Rorschach Data

- Rorschach data should be used to generate *hypotheses* about the examinee.
- These *hypotheses* should be integrated with data from other sources, such as other tests and structured interviews, life-history data, and data from collateral sources.
- Rorschach results can be simplified if the examiner attends closely to the referral question.
- RIAP or ROR-SCAN interpretive statements should not be quoted verbatim or extensively in a report.
- When the computer-generated statements are reviewed, they should be compared to each other because they are sometimes contradictory.

and thematic preoccupations. The Rorschach may be better than any other commonly used instrument in illustrating the quality and content of a thought disorder, and the Exner Special Scores provide a way to categorize how thought is disturbed.

Because the scores of the Rorschach contrast logical thinking with the experience and modulation of emotion, the Rorschach is also useful in evaluating the experience, expression, and control of emotion, as the examinee moves from the bland or "popular" percepts to those that are experienced as emotionally provocative or disturbing. There are several Exner scores that allow us to make statements about the examinee's capacity for control and stress tolerance. The Rorschach has been used less often to evaluate capacity for treatment or changes in treatment, yet there are variables that have emerged as important to treatment. This chapter will illustrate some of these clinical applications.

Rorschach data, like information from an MMPI or other psychological measure, is meant to be integrated with data from other sources, for example, life-history data, Mental Status Examination, and collateral sources, and should be used to generate hypotheses about the examinee. The computer-generated RIAP or ROR-SCAN interpretive statements should be regarded as *hypotheses* and not quoted extensively in a report. The same is true for hand-generated hypotheses. This chapter selects a few basic sets of Rorschach data to illustrate how variables and variable clusters are clinically meaningful. Caution 7.1 highlights tips for using Rorschach data.

ASSESSING WORLDVIEW AND SELF- AND OBJECT-REPRESENTATIONS

In the most concrete sense, worldview and life experience is conveyed by the content of a Rorschach. However, because this lends itself to a certain degree of "arm-chair" psychologizing, it is important that a review of the examinee's content be tied to a quantitative analysis of Rorschach results, and this is relatively easy to do using Exner's published tables of variables for "normals" and different diagnostic groups. The Exner Comprehensive System provides the following variables that assess self-representations:

- Egocentricity Index (3r + (2)/R)
- Reflections (Fr + rF)
- FD
- V
- Pure H:Non–Pure H
- An + Xy
- MOR
- Content of minus responses
- Content of movement responses

Another set of Exner variables address object representations:

- Food
- Texture (T)
- Hypervigilence Index
- COP
- AG
- H and H:Hd
- M, especially Mu and M–
- Content of human responses

A typical referral question surrounds an examinee's relationships and capacity for aggression. The following data are of a female stalker who we will call Pam (not her real name). Pam was arrested after breaking into her former boyfriend's apartment, stealing his address book, and making threatening calls to his mother and current girlfriend. Her scores are contrasted to the mean scores from Exner's data on nonpatient adults (see Exner, 1993). Note:

Standard deviations for this sample appear in parentheses; however, Exner (in workbook, 1990) notes that standard deviations for Rorschach variables may be misleading because some are not normally distributed, and they should not be used to calculate ranges.

First, we consider the examinee's self-perception (see Rapid Reference 7.1).

Self-Representations/Self-Perception

	Examinee	Adult Nonpt. Mean (S.d.)
Egocentricity Index (3r + (2)/R)	.44	.39 (.07)
Reflections (Fr + rF)	2	.08 (.35)
FD	0	1.16 (.87)
V	1	0.26 (.58)
Pure H:Non–Pure H	3:12	3.39 (1.80): 2.03 (–)
An + Xy	0	.45 (–)
MOR	1	.70 (.82)
Content of minus responses	mostly human	

The difference between the examinee and the adult normative sample may seem minimal, but a careful analysis reveals important dynamics of her relatedness. Although the examinee's Egocentricity Index is not significantly greater than the mean for adult nonexaminees, it is composed of two Reflection responses.

Reflections are more common in the records of children (e.g., 32% of the records of five year olds, 8% of the records of 11 year olds, 14% at age 14) but usually disappear during adolescence (Exner, volume 1, 3rd ed., p. 432). Reflections occur in roughly 7% of the adult nonexaminee sample but are more common in the records of patients. Exner (1998) reports that Reflections are present in 10% of the records of depressed patients and 13% of the schizophrenia sample (p. 433). Like the data of Gacano and Meloy (1994), Exner's character-disordered sample has the greatest number of Reflections, about 20%, a finding that has been replicated in the research with male stalkers and sexually aggressive psychopaths. Gacano, Meloy, and Berg (1992) found that 50% of psychopaths have at least one Reflection response, and of the groups of men diagnosed Narcissistic and Borderline, 50% and 33% of the records contain at least one Reflection. Berg, Gacano, Meloy, and Peaslee (1944) looked at women diagnosed Borderline and found that only 28% of the records contained a Reflection response. The earliest research on the Reflection score was analog. Jones (1965) explored the relationship between the use of personal pronouns on the Sentence Completion Blank and

≡ Rapid Reference 7.1

Pertinent Questions about Self

- How does the examinee see him- or herself?
- Is there too much or too little self-focus?
- Is the sense of self damaged?
- Is there too much negative self-evaluation occurring?
- Are there preoccupations in self-concept?

the occurrence of Reflections on the Rorschach. Eighty subjects from a larger sample were selected, 40 with the highest number of "I" statements (high S) and 40 with the lowest number (low S). Reflection responses appeared in the records of 37 of the 40 subjects from the "high S" group.

The Reflection tendency is relatively stable in the records of adults. For example, Exner (1998) reports on a study that examined the records of 100 non-patients retested after three years and 50 nonpatients retested after one year. Seventeen subjects gave at least one Reflection response in the first testing, and all 17 gave at least one Reflection response in their second testing.

A basic interpretive statement that could be drawn from Pam's Reflection responses is that she has a tendency to be quite self-focused. Similar individuals are said to have an increased need for frequent reaffirmation. They have considerable motives for status, and failure to obtain gratification of these ego needs may lead to behaviors or defense mechanisms that will protect the sense of self. They may have more concern for their own needs than the needs of others. Sometimes individuals like this are called "entitled" because they feel (or act like) their needs are more important than the needs of others. This narcissistic-like tendency makes it difficult to maintain close relationships. When the fragile sense of "self" is threatened, this person may resort to extreme needs to maintain their sense of self or to respond to a perceived "wound." Psychological defenses of rationalization, externalization, and denial may be seen.

Rapid Reference 7.2

Pertinent Questions about How the Examinee Sees Others

- Does the examinee have human content in his or her record?
- Is it whole human content or is there a tendency to see part-humans?
- Does the examinee seem isolated? Does he or she expect positive interaction?
- Is human interaction unusual? It is aggressive? Is it cooperative?
- Does the examinee seem excessively needy?

The nonpatient adult sample has more whole human percepts than part-human. The examinee, however, has a tendency to see part-human percepts rather than whole human percepts. She is inclined to be quite involved in fantasy. Similar individuals are said to have distorted notions about themselves and others.

Pam has one Morbid response. While this is not a dramatic difference in comparison to the normative sample, it suggests that she may brood about aspects of her "self" that she perceives as undesirable. The Morbid score was found in a response that seems fairly clearly to be a "projection," because of its elaboration:

(Card VI) Upside down it would be the same fur modeled by a woman with thin legs and wild hose, but with a head either obstructed by a coat, or they've taken her head off the picture, imaged it off, or something. The fur is the same as above. Legs coming down, toes pointed and wearing psychedelic wild tights because there is not one color and they have a pattern. It's like a tie-dye thing. In the middle it looks like a zipper.
Score: W + YF.TF _ H 25 MOV

In the vernacular, she feels like a headless "freak." It is probably no accident that this response also contains the Texture score, which is empirically related to the need for closeness and affection. As we will see when we review the "interpersonal perception" constellation of scores, below, the examinee combines a high state of need with a sense of "entitlement."

Next we consider how the Examinee perceives others (see Rapid Reference 7.2).

Other-Representations/Interpersonal Perception

	Examinee	Mean/Nonpt. Adults (S.d.)
Food	1	.23 (.50)
Texture	5	1.03 (.58)
Hypervigilence index	Neg	–
PER	2	1.05 (1.00)
COP	2	2.07 (1.52)
AG	2	1.18 (1.18)
A:P	11:7	6.48 (2.14):2.69 (1.52)
Isol:R	.06	.20 (.09)
Content of Movement responses with pairs		
All Human Content		

In terms of a comparison with nonpatient adults, the most striking feature of this protocol is the proliferation of Texture responses. The average non-patient adult has one Texture response; 89 percent of all subjects in the nonpatient normative sample gave at least one Texture response. The maximum value from the norms for adult nonpatients is 3 Texture. Exner and Bryant (1974) compared a sample of 30 recently separated or divorced subjects to demographically matched controls and found mean Texture scores of 3.57 and 1.31, respectively. Twenty-one of the 30 separated or divorced subjects were retested after six months. These 21 had averaged 3.49 Texture answers in the first test, but 2.64 in the second test. Leura and Exner (1976) compared 32 foster children, aged 7 to 11, who had no placement lasting longer than 14 months and a control group of 32 children who had lived with their own parents since birth. The mean for the foster children was .045, and 20 of these children had records with no T. Compare this to a mean of 1.47 for the control group children; only three of these children had records with no Texture. Exner points out that subjects with no Texture may have a need for closeness, but they appear to have stopped looking to the world for affectionate gratification. At any rate, they are typically described as more guarded or concerned with issues of personal space. Individuals who are above the mean, that is, who have more than one Texture response, have greater needs for closeness and probably feel quite lonely.

The examinee has a marked tendency to respond to the tactile qualities of the inkblots, and empirically this is associated with a strong need for affective closeness. The RIAP interpretive statement drawn from this score is, "She is a lonely person with a strong need for closeness. These . . . intense needs may have been provoked by a recent emotional loss, but they may represent a more chronic state that might have been initiated by a loss or disappointment and perpetuated because the loss was never compensated or replaced."

This examinee has a lot of human content in her record. The RIAP narrative states, "She has a very strong interest in people. This is generally a positive finding and suggests that she will usually seek out contacts with others." However, at the same time, she has a considerable capacity for distortion in her percepts of humans (two M– responses), and the interpretive statement continues: "Unfortunately, she does not have a very good understanding of people and this can often lead to naïve expectations concerning social relation" (RIAP, 1995). She also seems unsure about how to view human interaction. She has two cooperative movement responses and two aggressive movement responses. She may see the potential for cooperative interactions with others, but she also anticipates and possibly scans for aggressive potential. She may have the potential for "splitting," a psychodynamic description that indicates the tendency to see others (and oneself) as "all good" or "all bad." It is here that a review of the content of these responses illustrates how she views relationships with others. Her Human Content includes:

- Two Chinese warriors, mirroring each other, in conflict, bleeding, "but the rest of their body is more peaceful"
- Two men sparring, kickboxing, hurting each other
- Women from a third world country
- African boys
- A Bigfoot character
- A woman in a fur with thin legs and wild hosiery, without a head
- Little girls on a teeter totter
- An abstract painting of a man
- A clown with Bozo-type hair
- The back of a big woman, dressed in a corset

- A psychedelic man with hot-pink hair
- The psychedelic man's wife

Only three of her percepts would be scored H, for whole human content. Most of her "humans" are fantasy figures or are distanced from the contemporary or realistic self. This result also leads to the Exner Comprehensive interpretive statement that she probably does not have a very good understanding of people.

There are many more features of this examinee's Rorschach that could be interpreted. For example, her re-

Rapid Reference 7.3

Pertinent Questions about Emotion

- Is emotion a core element in decision making?
- When emotion is experienced, does it overrule logical thinking?
- Is there evidence of an unusual frequency of negative emotions?
- Are feelings controlled effectively?
- Is the examinee confused about his or her feelings?

ality testing is quite poor (X + % = .44 and X − % = .25), and there is consider-able data about affective disruption. The self- and object-representation analysis, however, had given us a considerable amount of information about the dynam-ics of her stalking of her ex-boyfriend. These indices suggest that her stalking stems from her overwhelming need for closeness plus her sense of entitlement.

ASSESSING EMOTION: CAPACITY FOR CONTROL AND STRESS TOLERANCE

When we assess emotion with the Rorschach, we are looking at the types of emotion manifested in Rorschach scores, for example, anger, anxiety, depres-sion, mixed painful states. We are looking at emotional control or the capac-ity for control. We are also looking for clinical/diagnostic signs of intense emotion or emotional dyscontrol. Some of the specific questions the Ror-schach can answer are, Is emotion a core element in decision making? Is there evidence of an unusual frequency of negative emotions? Are feelings con-trolled effectively? Is the examinee confused about his feelings? (See Rapid Reference 7.3.) Pertinent variables here include:

- EB (Sum of M:Sum of Color)
- Eb (FM+m:C', T, V, Y)
- EA : es

- FC:CF + C
- Pure C
- Afr
- S
- Blends
- Color Projection
- Color-Shading Blends
- Shading Blends

It is important, first, to examine potentially dangerous clinical states. Several special indices have been developed for assessing clinical depression and suicide potential. The Depression Index (DEPI) is comprised of the following variables and is considered positive if the examinee has five or more variables:

- FV + VF + V > 0 or FD >2
- Color-Shading Blends > 0 or S > 2
- Egocentricity > .44 + Fr + rF = 0 or Egocentricity < .33
- Afr < .46 or Blends < 4
- Sum of Shading > FM + m or Sum C' > 2
- Mor > 2 or 2AB + Art + Ay > 3
- COP < 2 or Isolate/R > .24

To the new Rorschach user, this set of variables may seem unnecessarily complex, but they are calculated by the computer (RIAP-4 or ROR-SCAN) and they are based on empirical studies. A simple statement if the examinee is positive on DEPI is that this examinee has many features in common with patients who are seriously depressed. The same is true for S-Con, which was developed out of research with attempted and effected suicides in patients who were tested because they were depressed.

The variables in the S-Con include:

- FV + VF + V + FD > 2
- Color-Shading Blends > 0
- 3r + (2)R < .31 or > .44
- MOR > 3
- Zd > +3.5 or Zd < −3.5
- es > EA
- CF + C > FC
- X+% < .70
- S > 3

- P < 3 or P > 8
- Pure H < 2
- R < 17

Once the crucial variables assessing clinical depression and suicide potential have been examined, the capacity for control and stress tolerance can be reviewed. Variables pertinent to the capacity for control and stress tolerance are:

- EA (Sum M plus the Sum of all color): Exner considers this an amalgamation of resources available for problem-solving.
- es (FM + m, plus T, V, C', and Y): These are the variables which create an internal state of dysphoria and distress and internal tension.
- D: This score is calculated by subtracting es from EA, then entering the Table 10 in the Rorschach workbook (5th Edition), to determine the D score.
- Adjusted D: This score is calculated by taking out all but one *m* and all but one Y from the es, then recalculating EA–es, and re-entering Table 10 for a new D score.

It should be obvious that a person who has a high degree of internal distress and tension and a limited number of resources with which to deal with these painful emotions will have poor stress tolerance and may be either situationally or chronically in stress overload. The D score reflects the examinee's current ability to cope with their amount of experienced distress. Adjusted D reflects how they might look if current stressors are subtracted from the picture.

Other variables that address the question of coping resources are Lambda and the Coping Deficit Index. Lambda is important in evaluating coping because a high Lambda score suggests a narrow, form-based, or constricted approach to the test. While this may be simple defensiveness, it is possible or even likely that the examinee takes this approach to many tasks. The Coping Deficit Index was empirically derived and individuals with CDI > 4 were described as limited in coping abilities (see Rapid Reference 7.4).

≡ *Rapid Reference 7.4*

The Coping Deficit Index

1. EA < 6 or Ajd D < 0
2. COP < 2 and AG < 2
3. Weighted Sum C < 2.5 or Afr < .46
4. Passive > Active + 1 or Pure H < 2
5. Sum T > 1 or ISOL. > .24 or Food > 0

The case of Gary illustrates the use of these variables to assess emotion, it's manifestation and control, and general coping abilities. Gary was admitted to an outpatient setting after several attempts by his family to admit him to an inpatient facility. Twenty-four years old, he began to show signs of serious depression when his wife filed for divorce and began to date others. He seemed to be obsessed regarding the safety of his two small daughters and the life they might have with a stepfather. The examinee attributed his divorce to his wife's friendship with a particular girlfriend, but in reality, there was a history of domestic violence, spurred by the examinee's jealousy and his wife was struggling to get away from him. She had moved out shortly before Christmas. The examinee was living in the couple's home, but said he could "hardly stand to be there" without his wife and daughters and came home only every few days to shower and pet his cat. When not at home, he slept in his car. He quit his job, stating he couldn't bear to have his coworkers ask him how he was doing. During the day, he often parked outside a previous job site, usually a house he and his coworkers had finished, so that he could recall happier times. The examinee developed a significant sleep disorder. Unknown to his family, he was consuming a pint of hard liquor a day, he said, to help him sleep. Shortly after the Christmas holidays, the examinee attempted suicide. He was drinking heavily and had shaved his head. His family took him to a county facility, which released him the following morning. He said he had to sleep on the cold cement floor and he would not go back to a hospital. Several days later, he was found hiding in the closet in his home, disheveled and frightened. His family then brought him for outpatient evaluation. Because of his history of domestic violence and his desperation about the loss of his wife and daughters, the evaluation was focused on affect, controls, and stress tolerance.

It is instructive to take the components of these indices and look at them separately. This kind of review teaches us about some of these variables.

Variables related to emotion	Examinee	Nonpatient Adults
EB (Sum of M:Sum of Color)	7:6.5	4.3 (.19):4.52 (1.79)
eb (Sum of FM + m: Sum C'T, V, Y)	14:19	4.82 (1.52):3.39 (2.15)
FC:CF + C	3:5	4.09 (1.88):2.44 (.28)
Pure C	0	.08 (.28)
Afr	.41	.69 (.16)
S	4	1.47 (1.21)

Blends	15	5.16 (1.93)
Color Projection	0	.02 (.28)
Color-Shading Blends	4	.46 (.69)
Shading Blends	2	–

EB is a ratio contrasting the balance between logical, form-based responses and those that incorporate color (FC, CF, and Pure C). At first glance, it seems that the examinee is well balanced here. He has a good deal of M, which Exner describes as "probably the subject of more investigations than any other Rorschach determinant" (p. 416, Exner, 1993) and related to intellectual operations and problem-solving ability. The examinee's M's are almost all unusual or minus in Form Quality, suggesting that whatever capacity for problem solving he had is very compromised. When color is examined (FC:CF + C is 3:5), it seems clear that his experience of strong emotion disrupts logical thinking. Examinee's Affective Ratio (Afr) indicates he tries to back away from the experience of strong emotion. The RIAP narrative states, "He has a marked tendency to avoid emotional stimuli. People such as this usually are quite uncomfortable around emotion and as a result, often become much more socially constrained or even isolated." His need to back away from emotion is probably based on his awareness that he becomes overwhelmed with pain and this is quite destabilizing.

The ratio eb (FM + m:Sum Shading) is somewhat different than EB. Both sides of this ratio reflect the internal pressure on a person. FM + m is related to need states. The score m or "little m" as it is sometimes called, is empirically associated with helplessness and the perception that one is controlled by outside forces. The Sum of Shading is associated with painful internal states. Y is empirically associated with anxiety, T with the need for affectionate closeness, V with introspection, and C' with dysphoria. In this examinee's case, he has 8 m's, 4 C' responses, 2 Texture responses, 1 Vista response, and *12* Y responses. To begin with, he feels a profound loss of control over what happens to him and is overwhelmed by his own helplessness (m = 8). He has very strong needs for affective closeness (T = 2), which are probably greater now because of his current loss of his wife and daughters. He is currently engaged in painful introspection (V = 1 and one of his Color-Shading Blends included V). He feels a combination of intense sadness (C' = 4) and anxiety (Y = 12). He also experiences a good deal of anger (S = 4), which may be a chronic feature of his personality.

The examinee's Color-Shading Blends and his Shading Blends indicate he experiences two different, probably contradictory feelings. The RIAP interpretive narrative states, "He is often confused by emotion and experiences both positive and negative feelings in response to the same stimulus situation. People such as this often experience feelings more intensely than others and sometimes have more difficulty in bringing emotional situations to closure." Examinee has a very large number of Blends (15 overall, 5 of which involve color and shading). At a minimum, it could be said that the examinee has considerable difficulty processing his experience in a simple, logical way. The computer narrative about his Blend tendency states, "His psychological functioning is more complex than ordinarily expected and involves considerable emotion. At times his psychological functioning is inordinately complex, which is almost always the result of emotional experience."

Perhaps the best summary statement about the examinee's affect from the computer narrative is:

> He is in considerable subjectively felt distress. Some of this discomfort is being created by situationally-related stress. Some of this distress includes marked feelings of loneliness and/or grief concerning a significant emotional loss. Part of his discomfort stems from feelings created by his tendency to ruminate about personal characteristics that he perceives as being undesirable. Some of this rumination appears to be provoked by feelings of guilt, shame, or remorse. Some of the distress is related to his tendency to hold in many feelings that he would prefer to release openly.

The computer-scored protocol highlights the fact that the examinee is positive on S-Con (10 variables, where the cutting score is 8 variables). He is also positive on DEPI (6 variables, where the cutting score is 5). The first statement in the computer-generated narrative is, "His protocol contains many features similar to those found among people with chronic and serious affective disorders." Exner's research on suicide and the development of S-Con is particularly important here. Exner (1978, volume 2) examined the records of 59 examinees who had committed suicide within 60 days of the time they were tested with the Rorschach and compared them with 31 records collected within 60 days of a suicide attempt and 33 records collected five days after a suicide attempt, as well as the records of 50 depressed inpatients, 50 inpatient schizophrenics, and

50 nonpatients. Subdividing the records of the suicides and attempted suicides by lethality of method, and performing a discriminent function analysis, he derived the 11 variables of S-Con. When he used these variables to determine their accuracy in predicting suicide, he found that if 8 variables of the constellation were positive, the "hit" rate for predicting suicide in the effectors' group was 75%. This cutting score also captures a significant proportion of the inpatient depressed group, that is, yielded "false positives," but it did not produce false positives among the nonpatient group. Exner cautioned that 25% of the completed suicide group did not have 8 variables of this constellation. The usefulness of S-Con probably varies with the richness of the Rorschach record. See Exner's discussion of how some of these individual affective variables may be related to serious depression (1978, pp. 207–8).

We have examined the examinee's emotions; now we turn to his ability to control strong emotion. Exner states that capacity for control is probably best defined as the ability to draw on available resources to formulate and implement deliberate behaviors designed to contend with situational demands. As the capacity for control increases, the ability to tolerate stress also increases. Examinee, as seen above, has a rather extraordinary amount of painful affect. Does he have the capacity to think about solutions? Does he have other emotional resources? His variables in this cluster are:

	Examinee	Adult Nonpatients
EA	13.5	8.82 (2.18)
es	33	8.21 (3.00)
D	−7	.04 (1.09)
Adj D	0	.20 (.88)
CDI	3	over 4 is significant

According to the RIAP interpretive statement:

He is experiencing a significant increase in stimulus demands as a result of situationally related stress. This has created considerable disorganization in his psychological operations and an extreme vulnerability to impulsive thinking, emotion, and behavior. He is likely to exhibit problems in attention, concentration, and following through on planned behaviors. These can occur even in structured situations. Ideational controls may be more impaired than is customary. There may be greater problems in judgment than are usually present. There is clearly a potential for impulsive-like behaviors.

It is interesting to note that the examinee's MMPI profile is most elevated on Scales 7 and 8 (T = 96). A standard text on the MMPI-2 (Graham, 1990) states: "These individuals are typically in a great deal of turmoil. They are not hesitant to admit to psychological problems, and they seem to lack adequate defenses to keep them reasonably comfortable. They report feeling depressed, worried, tense, and nervous." MMPI-2 Scale 2 is elevated at 84, which is objectively high and should trigger concern about suicide potential. When all of the Rorschach data on the examinee is analyzed, the need for immediate intervention is clear. He is likely in a Major Depressive Episode and he should be followed closely due to his previous history of domestic violence and other dramatic acts.

ASSESSING CAPACITY TO BENEFIT FROM TREATMENT AND THERAPY RESPONSE

The Rorschach can be used to explore variables associated with motivation for treatment, capacity to benefit from treatment, and progress in treatment (see Rapid Reference 7.5). While it is tempting to evaluate the progress of examinees by using simple checklists such as the Beck, the Rorschach given over time can measure structural changes in personality that are often the primary target of intensive psychotherapy.

Hilsenroth, Handler, Toman, and Padawer (1995) explored the Rorschach's potential to discriminate between examinees who stayed in treatment and those who did not. Looking at 97 examinees who prematurely terminated psychotherapy and 81 who participated in individual psychotherapy for at least six months, they found significant differences in Rorschach scores COP,

Rapid Reference 7.5

Questions Pertinent to Evaluating Need for Treatment

- How does the examinee manage stress?
- What is the examinee's typical coping style? Is this adaptive?
- Can the patient examine him- or herself?
- Does the patient feel comfortable with others?

AG, and T. Interestingly, examinees who terminated psychotherapy prematurely were found to have fewer Texture responses, more Cooperative Movement (COP) responses, and fewer Aggressive Movement (AG) responses, compared with those who stayed in treatment. Examinees with more T were hypothesized to be more needy and therefore more likely to stay in treatment as a way of meeting their needs for affective closeness. Terminating examinees seemed healthier (i.e., more COP and less AG), and it was hypothesized that they may have concluded that their social support networks provided more meaningful support than psychotherapy. The MMPI's of these groups were not significantly different, even on the TRT scale (Negative Treatment Indicators), which is purported to be a treatment prognostic scale.

Weiner and Exner (1991) suggest several constellations of Rorschach variables for use in evaluating response to treatment, drawing from texts on dynamic psychotherapy. Goals of dynamic and other therapies include learning to adequately manage stress, developing a consistent coping style, attending openly to experiences, engaging in constructive self-examination, and feeling comfortable in interpersonal relationships. The following variables are suggested for each characteristic:

Stress Management

$D < 0$	Subjectively felt distress resulting from inadequate resources to meet demands
Adj $D < 0$	Persistently felt distress extending beyond transient or situational difficulties
$EA < 7$	Limited resources for implementing deliberate strategies of resolving problematic situations
$CDI > 3$	General deficit in capacities for coping with demands of daily living

Developing a Consistent Coping Style

Ambitence	Lack of commitment to a cohesive coping style
$Zd < -3.0$	Insufficient attention to the nuances of experience, superficial scanning of environment, hastily drawn conclusions
Lambda $> .99$	Narrow and limited frames of reference and an inclination to respond to situations in the simplest possible terms

Developing a Consistent Coping Style   continued

X+% < .70	Inability to perceive objects and events as most people would
X–% > .20	Inaccurate perception and faulty anticipation of the consequences of actions

Modulating Emotion

CF + C > FC + 1	Intensity of affect and the degree to which it is controlled by logic
Sum Shading> FM + m	Negative emotional experience of dysphoria, loneliness, helplessness
Afr < .50	Unwillingness to become involved in affect-laden situations
DEPI ≥ 5	Presence of variables associated with depression

Problems Examining Oneself

Fr + rF > 0	Narcissistic tendencies and projection of blame
3r + (2)/R > .43	Excessive self-focus and preoccupation with oneself
3r + (2)/R < .33	Low regard for oneself in comparison with others
FD > 2	Unusual extent of introspection

Difficulty Feeling Comfortable in Interpersonal Relationships

P > a + 1	Passivity in relation to other people, avoidance of responsibility and initiative taking
T = 0	Lack of expectation or reaching out for close, psychologically intimate, nurturant, and mutually supportive relationships
T > 1	Unmet needs for close and comforting relationships with others, loneliness and deprivation
Pure H < 2	Disinterest in and/or difficulty identifying with other people
H < [(H) + Hd + (Hd)]	Uneasiness in contemplating relationships with real, live, and fully functional people

The following case illustrates the use of these variables to evaluate progress in psychotherapy. The examinee has had persistent difficulties relating to men. She tends to choose partners who are physically abusive, and when these relationships are over, she feels devastated. At these times, she can be self-destructive and angry. She was tested in the initial phase of treatment, which was at a time of acute turmoil at the end of a relationship, and two years later, after weekly intensive psychodynamic psychotherapy.

A comparison of these two points in time on the variables suggested by Exner and Weiner (1991) was conducted. The examinee was only positive on the "Stress Management" variable D < O at the first testing. Despite the fact that she was positive on S-Con and DEPI and appeared to be severely clinical depressed and thought-disordered, D was only −1. This was nevertheless suggestive of a considerable amount of subjectively felt stress. However, at the second testing 2 years later, D was 0 and Adj D was +1.

The variable cluster evaluating coping style at Time 1 revealed that this examinee was an Ambitent (EB = 7:8), and at Time 2 she was Introversive (EB = 8:4). While this woman has superior intelligence and is a creative and intuitive woman, the right side of her EB before therapy is made up largely of M− responses (4 M− and 3 Mu). By the second testing, this score has changed somewhat. She has 8 M's — 3 are M−, 3 are Mu, and 2 are Mo. This distribution reflects at least some improvement in her ability to see people more realistically and engage less in fantasy and projection, but continuing therapy should focus on realistic perceptions of others.

With the variable cluster "Modulating Emotion," the greatest change appears to be a dimunution of anger. At Time 1, S = 5, whereas at Time 2, S = 2. She is somewhat more willing to experience, rather than avoid, affect. Afr at Time 1 is .27 and at Time 2 is .57. Hopefully, this is the result of a type of therapy that has focused on learning how to tolerate and move through the experience of painful affect.

There are some important changes in the variables about self and others, as well. In the first testing, she had one Reflection response but her Egocentricity Index was quite low (.32). She also had a Vista response. Clearly, she was in a painful state of looking inward and evaluating herself quite negatively. After two years of psychotherapy, her Vista scores disappeared, as did her Reflection. Her Egocentricity Index was .64. While this probably still does not reflect good self-esteem and likely involves too much self-focus, she was clearly not as vulnerable and regressed as at Time 1. Regarding relationships with other, at the second testing, she had gone from 2 Texture responses, to

Table 7.1   Evaluating Treatment

	Time 1 (beginning of treatment)	Time 2 (after 2 years of treatment)
Stress Management		
$D < 0$	yes	no
Adj $D < 0$	no	no
$EA < 7$	no	no
$CDI > 3$	no	no
Coping Style		
Ambitence	yes	no
$Zd < -3.0$	no	no
Lambda $> .99$	no	no
$X +\% < .70$	yes	yes
$X -\% > .20$	yes	yes
Modulating Emotion		
$CF + C > FC + 1$	yes	yes
Sum Shading $> FM + m$	yes	no
Afr $< .50$	yes	no
$DEPI \geq 5$	yes	no
Problems Examining Self		
$Fr + rF > 0$	yes	no
$3r + (2)/R > .43$	no	yes
$3r + (2)R < .33$	yes	no
$FD > 2$	no	no

Table 7.1   continued

Difficulty in Interpersonal Relationships

p > a + 1	no	no
T = 0	yes (T = 2)	no (T = 1)
T > 1	yes (T = 2)	no (T = 1)
Pure H < 2	no	no
H < [(H) + Hd + (Hd)]	yes	no

one, and her active to passive ratio was similar, with a preference for active over passive responding. The most important change was in the perception of others, captured by Pure H and Whole H:All Other H. The latter ratio changed from 3:6 to 6:3. This finding is similar to the reduction in M– responses and reflects a better capacity to accurately perceive others, which was the theoretical basis of the therapy (with an object relations focus).

Perhaps the most overt sign that this examinee had benefited from treatment was the fact that, at Time 2, her S-Con and DEPI constellations were not positive. Testing this examinee a second time with the Rorschach, after two years of therapy, highlighted areas of her functioning that were yet unchanged and would be the focus of continuing therapy.

 TEST YOURSELF

1. **Important clinical uses of the Rorschach are**
    (a) to evaluate reality-testing.
    (b) to evaluate emotional control.
    (c) to evaluate relationships with others.
    (d) to evaluate aspects of change in therapy.
    (e) all of the above.

2. **Variables that are useful in evaluating emotion and emotional control are**

   (a) FC CF + C.

   (b) S.

   (c) Afr.

   (d) F+%.

   (e) a, b, & c.

3. **The capacity for control is important in evaluating ability to cope with stress because it is a way of evaluating the resources the examinee can bring to bear to cope with situational demands.** True or False?

4. **Rorschach variables or constellations which may be useful in evaluating progress in therapy are**

   (a) stress management.

   (b) coping style.

   (c) modulating emotion.

   (d) comfort in interpersonal relationships.

   (e) all of the above.

Answers: 1. e; 2. e; 3. true; 4. e.

Eight

ILLUSTRATIVE CASE REPORT

Nancy Kaser-Boyd, Ph.D.

hapters 1 through 6 have reviewed key features of administration, scoring, and interpretation of the Rorschach. This chapter will demonstrate how hypotheses are cross-validated with behavioral observations, background information, and other psychological tests. It will illustrate how to sort through the complex and sometimes contradictory interpretive hypotheses and write about a person in a way that makes sense to the referral source and is connected to recommendations. This chapter brings together the principles from previous chapters and culminates in the presentation of two sample reports. This case was selected because of the richness of the Rorschach protocol and because the assessment was conducted in one of the common arenas where reports are written to nonpsychologists and must be clear and simple.

ILLUSTRATIVE CASE REPORT: MARIA

Maria was referred by the Court after she was arrested for assault resulting from an incident with her boyfriend. He believed she had been stalking him and that she was obsessed with him. She reported a history of emotional and sexual abuse by this man, and the incident that led to her arrest was preceded by several months of psychological deterioration, which included sleep impairment, weight loss, and religious preoccupation. She would stay up late at night composing religious writing. In order to be able to fall asleep, she often engaged in self-hypnosis, which was self-taught and involved morbid fantasies of death. The referral questions included Examinee's mental state at the time of the offense, her treatment needs, and the likelihood that she would act similarly if released.

Examinee was a 41-year-old Anglo woman, a high school graduate who had traveled around the world and developed her own business. The mother of two latency-aged children, she had been divorced for several years. At the age of 19, she had been viciously raped by a stranger and had received only brief crisis counseling. Approximately one year prior to her assault on her boyfriend, while on a ski weekend, she sustained second degree burns on her face after a gas oven she was lighting exploded. She was not able to work after this accident. Her boyfriend, whom she had been supporting, subsequently moved out. Her symptoms became evident soon after his departure. Examinee had one previous episode of depression, with suicidal ideation, after a previous break-up several years prior.

Table 8.1 provides Maria's Rorschach protocol. Examinee became upset by the Rorschach cards, beginning at Card II, when she began to cry and said, "These cards are really upsetting me. Are they supposed to make me feel like this?" She had difficulty taking distance from the inkblots, commenting to Card IX, "This reminds me of me when I had bulimia," and adding at the end of the test that the cat on Card II reminded her of her ex-boyfriend. Examinee also completed the Minnesota Multiphasic Personality Inventory (MMPI-2) and the Millon Clinical Multiaxial Inventory (MCMI-III). Tables 8.2 and 8.3 list Maria's Sequence of Scores and Structural Summary.

The first step in Rorschach interpretation is a consideration of validity. The number of responses and the Lambda score are crucial validity indicators. A record that is less than 14 responses is not typically considered valid. Although it will provide some data about the current state of the examinee, there will likely be insufficient data to make statements about "personality." The Examinee had 19 responses, which is within the normal range. Lambda should fall within the range of .59 and .94. Persons with Lambda scores of .99 or greater have mostly used form in their responses, and these records tell us little about personality. Lambda scores of .59 or less are seen in those who are very influenced by emotion. Examinee's record is valid and should be interpretively useful.

The computerized interpretive report (RIAP-4) generated 37 hypotheses about Examinee, some of which directly contradicted each other. The RIAP-4 interpretive hypotheses are meant to be clinician-to-clinician consultation, and a good report should not quote extensively from them. Instead, the Structural Summary should be reviewed and the most relevant variables

Table 8.1   Rorschach Protocol—Maria

Free Association	Inquiry
I. 1. This looks like a woman's pelvis.	This here looks like a spine, and this looks like bones . . . down here it looks like the opening to the uterus . . . and up here possibly a womb. Up here it could be the opening to the cervix, the shape right here, the curvature, and that it's overlying or underlying here makes it look like a bone structure. [Overlying?] Like I'm looking at it from the rear, the way the bones cut across and cut into the surface. [?] Because it's darker.
2. It looks like a beautiful, exotic bug.	These would be two little claws and this would be the head. This would be wings outspread, but not normal wings, because they have an open, airy part, parts to them (Points to spaces). [Beautiful?] Because of the open, airy wings . . . even his head is different, not just one head . . . it looks exotic, almost deformed, but beautiful.
II. 3. Looks like a cat kissing a window . . . it's pretty horrifying looking . . .	It looks like he ate something that's really bloody, or ate a hole in something that's bloody. His paws are on the top of it, and they are bloody, too. This represents a chin, with blood dripping down and blood on paws, paws holding on to everything he's eating. The cat looks demonic. [?] I guess the fact that it has two eyes and it's as if it has no conscience . . . like it's empty, just doing it for the rapture . . . the pure pleasure of it.
4. Looks like a ballet dancer, a large ballet dancer . . .	These look like her feet . . . she's on her toes and this is her torso . . . I don't know why it (the body) would be open in the middle . . . maybe some sort of emblem, hanging on a chain. [You said it looks like her body is open in the middle?] Maybe her body is not present, just the pieces she wears, almost as if on a hanger.
5. I see it both ways (as a costume with a medallion and as a woman ripped apart with her heart torn out, and blood all over her clothes). I see it both ways, but it scares me this other way, so I said clothing on a hanger.	[Ripped apart?] Yes, looks like her heart was ripped out (space) and blood because it's red.

Table 8.1   continued

Free Association	Inquiry
III. 6. Looks like two people holding on to something and looks like their hearts have been torn out of their bodies, but they are connected . . . just like they are trying to pull away . . . Is this supposed to make me feel like this (beginning to cry, very upset). I feel very scared . . . I just see a lot of ugliness . . .	Looks like two people pulling, see here their bottom, almost like they are attached to something (here, pointing to D1 area) and can't get away, pulling and pulling, too tightly connected, almost looks like attached at the top, but an explosion tore them apart, but their hearts are still connected, and are out here. I keep wanting to say this is matter (pointing to the other red) like their minds have been hurt, too, and also looks like blood behind their heads.
7. It sort of looks like an X-ray of a child . . . somebody that's facing a wall and there is nothing inside, just a torn-up heart.	Just an X-ray that is transparent. [Transparent?] Yes, parts you can see in between, like you can see the bones, and you can see in between the bones.
IV. 8. I see a tree in a forest, like a fir tree and I see like a spirit attached to the tree kind of guarding, it's an ominous spirit, it says he is not going to let anything bad happen to the trees, it will take care of the forest.	Here is three trees, this darker part in the middle. Up here it is the wood spirit, and he's got big feet and these look like birds and everything is symbolic of blessing. It's dark and ominous, but something very gentle, loving, protective. [Dark?] All these different variations in grays and the levels of them, from lighter to darker.
9. This card is very fairytale-like, swans, a castle, clouds, looks like impending doom, but goodness. I see a lot of fantasy-oriented things, and these two things down here, they feel really good, like they symbolize something strange but good.	Impending doom because of the dark. Clouds because they are kind of dark on bottom and light on top. It might be even the color (gray), I'm not sure, but it looks like clouds over an ocean.
V. 10. Kind of reminds me of a cecropolis . . . a really beautiful moth from South America.	They are large . . . up to one foot across with enormous wings, and their antennae have large filament fibers and are very delicate and have a tail. They are very beautiful. This one isn't beautiful . . . I look at it and think "God! This is ugly." But the first thing I thought of was a cecropolis. Ugly and disturbing . . . it

Table 8.1   continued

Free Association	Inquiry
	makes my stomach hurt. I guess that's a more honest perception of it.
11. Physically it even looks like a bat.	A comic look to it, like a dancing bat in a strange costume, like a person in an opera . . . awkward wings, much too heavy to have to drag . . . a weird hat and furry little feet. [Furry?] Just do. Looks like if he tried to walk, he'd fall all over the place, almost like a burlesque bat.
12. This was the first thing that came to mind was that it was a smile, an artist's version of an abstract smile.	The bottom of the nose and going down through the chin.
VI. 13. It's like an American Indian, like a petroglyph or design. Even though it's very colorful to me. Looks like it could be ceremonial robe, more like a ceremonial robe, but beaded, perhaps used in certain rituals like a medicine man would . . . it's very pretty, beautiful, I mean . . .	More like in a healing ceremonial robe . . . the big skin of an animal and this part (top) had been purposely nicked away and beaded to fit on the head. [What makes it look like skin?] The center spine and you can tell it's lighter here and darker here, and a neck part comes up here, like if you sewed it together, it would actually look like a butt. [Colorful?] I can see blues and greens and reds toward the center and maybe even some black in there and some yellow.
14. The explosion of sperm in the uterus.	Just in my imagination, sperm will travel upward and when it hits the womb it would scatter. This seems like a canal with fluid rushing through it, and this looks like tissue structure. [?] The softness of it (touches it) like when you cut a fish, it looks fleshy and smooth.
VII. 15. Two children at odds with one another. They are the same, but they're not the same. They are attached, but it's not comfortable. They are struggling to get apart. There is great torment and no success, and a lot of decay and death.	The fact that it is all black and their mouths have all different levels of it, and everything is distorted, smudged, and smeared, and not clear. Looks like children, but they look so old and worn out.

Table 8.1   continued

Free Association	Inquiry
VIII. 16. This is an animal climbing over the rocks and looking at it's reflection in a pool of water below . . . looks like he's reaching out, looks like a lot of obstacles and hard things are in his way. Appears to be easy for him, but it's not. He may have to go back and go the other way.	Looks like it's leaving a forest or rocks. [Rocks?] Just the jaggedness of it, the formations of rocks. It can't get there, that is what forced it to see its reflection in the water, and it's realizing it's going to have to turn back. [Water?] The clearness here, and that there is an exact reflection of itself . . . how smooth it is.
IX. 17. Oh, this reminds me of my bulimia. Reminds me of someone bent over and vomiting . . . and no matter which way she turns she can't seem to control what's going on inside of her. You can see her insides here . . . they look pretty worn out.	Looking down at the colors of the different things that just came out. She is here and here (pointing to the symmetrical pair). [Did you say she?] Yes, she is back to back, as if everywhere she turns, and no matter what she did, it didn't matter, the same things would happen. This one almost looks angry, but this one just looks sad, in anguish, desperate, completely out of control, and the other one looks angry, she is throwing up her anger.
18. I see ugliness surrounding holiness, like a flame holding on to itself, but completely surrounded by ugliness. The colors are beautiful, but they seem really deceiving.	I see a flame right here, just seems spiritual . . . it's soft and glowing. [Soft and glowing?] Because it is a blue flame. Then I just see all this control and it is arrogant enough to stretch out the control without being burned by it. Laughing and not caring. Clothed in a nice color, but smeared. The ideas are ever present deep inside. Outside it appears to be wonderful, but it's not.
X. 19. This is like the 4th of July . . . but underwater, like little amoebas and creatures and seahorses, just I guess the symmetry and the beauty that is found naturally in nature . . . and two little creatures kissing in the middle.	To me it looks like a celebration, an explosion of something that is very controlled but nevertheless explodes. The clearness of the color and the smallness of the color is very gay and celebrative.

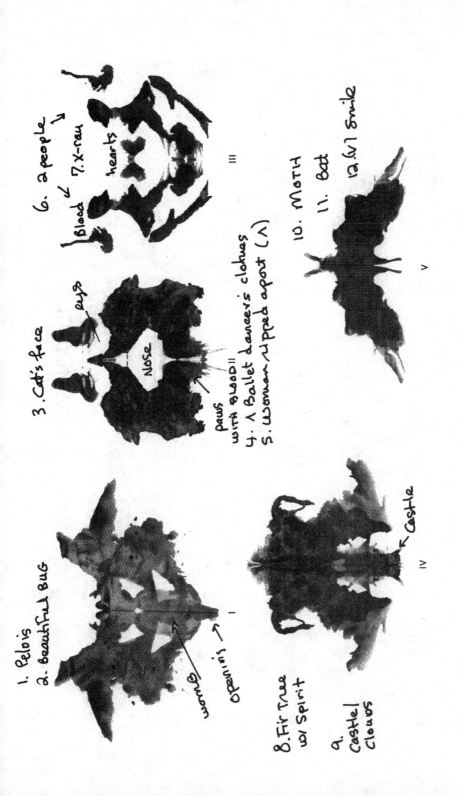

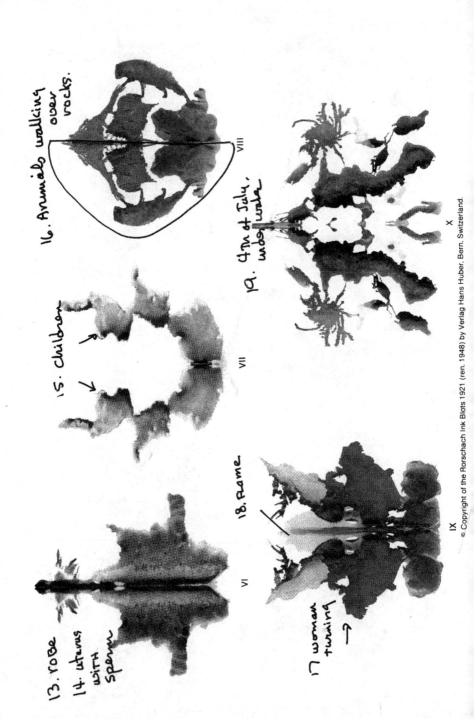

13. ROBE
14. uterus with sperm

VI

15. Children

VII

16. Animals walking over rocks.

VIII

18. flame

19. 4th of July. underwater.

X

17 woman turning

IX

© Copyright of the Rorschach Ink Blots 1921 (ren. 1948) by Verlag Hans Huber, Bern, Switzerland.

Table 8.2 Sequence of Scores, Maria

Client Name:

Client ID:

Gender: -Not specified-

Date of Birth: 05/28/1951

Test Date: 02/07/1992

Description:

Card	Resp. No	Location and DQ	Loc. No.	Determinant(s) and Form Quality	(2)	Contents	Pop	Z Score	Special Scores
I	1	WS+	1	FV+		Hd,Sx		4.0	
	2	WSo	1	FMpu		A		3.5	INC, MOR
II	3	WS+	1	Ma.mp.FC.FV−		A,Bl,Hx		4.5	AG, MOR, AB, DR2
	4	WS+	1	mp−		Cg,Art		4.5	
	5	WS+	1	Mp.CF−		Hd,Bl		4.5	MOR
III	6	W+	1	Mp.CF−	2	H,Bl,Ex,Hx	P	5.5	MOR, AB, DR2
	7	WS+	1	Mp.CF−		Hd,Xy		5.5	MOR, FAB2
IV	8	W+	1	Mp.YF−		(H),A,Bt		4.0	AB
	9	Wv/+	1	YF.C'F−		Cl,A,Na,Ay		4.0	AB, MOR, DR
V	10	Wo	1	Fo		A		1.0	DR2
	11	W+	1	Mau		(A),Cg		2.5	INC
	12	Wo	1	Mp−		Hd,Art		1.0	

Table 8.2 continued

Card	Resp. No	Location and DQ	Loc. No.	Determinant(s) and Form Quality	(2)	Contents	Pop	Z Score	Special Scores
VI	13	Wo	1	FY.FC'u		Ad,Ay		2.5	CP
	14	WS+	1	Ma.FT–		Hd,Sx		6.5	DV
VII	15	W+	1	Ma.FC'.FYo	2	H,Hx	P	2.5	MOR, AG, FAB2, AB
VIII	16	W+	1	FMa.Fro		A,Na	P	4.5	DR2
IX	17	W+	1	Ma.CF–		H,Hx,An		5.5	MOR, AG, PER, AB
	18	W+	1	Mp.ma–		Hx,Fi		5.5	AB, MOR
X	19	W+	1	Ma.ma.CFu	2	A,Ex,Na		5.5	DV, FAB2

Summary of Approach

I:	WS.WS	VI:	W.WS
II:	WS.WS.WS	VII:	W
III:	W.WS	VIII:	W
IV:	W.W	IX:	W.W
V:	W.W.W	X:	W

Protocol was scored by N. Kaser-Boyd and D. Viglione, Ph.D.

Table 8.2 continued

RIAP™ Structural Summary Report

Client Name: Maria
Client ID: 52851

Constellations Table

S-Constellation (Suicide Potential)	SCZI (Schizophrenia Index)
☐ Positive if 8 or more conditions are true:	☑ Positive if 4 or more conditions are true:
Note: Applicable only for subjects over 14 years old.	
☐ FV+VF+FD [2] > 2	☑ ((X + % [0.21] < 0.61) *and* (S–% [0.45] < 0.41)) *or* (X + % [0.21] < 0.50)
☑ Col-Shd Blends [1] > 0	☑ X – % [0.58] > 0.29
☐ Ego [0.32] < .31 *or* > .44	☑ (FQ – [11] ≥ FQu [4]) *or* (FQ–[11] > FQo [3] + FQ+ [1])
☑ MOR [9] > 3	☑ (Sum Level 2 Special Scores [7] > 1) *and* (FAB2 [3] > 0)
☑ Zd [14.0] > ±3.5	☑ (Raw Sum of 6 Special Scores [12] > 6) *or* (Weighted Sum of 6 Special Scores [54] > 17)

Table 8.2 continued

S-Constellation (Suicide Potential)

☑ es [16] > EA [17.5]

☑ CF + C [5] > FC [1]

☑ X+% [0.21] < .70

☑ S [7] > 3

☐ P [3] < 3 or > 8

☐ Pure H [3] < 2

☐ R [19] < 17

6　Total

SCZI (Schizophrenia Index)

☑ (M–[9] > 1) or (X – % [0.58] > 0.40

6　Total

DEPI (Depression Index)

☑ Positive if 5 or more conditions are true:

☑ (FV + VF + V [2] > 0) or (FD [0] > 2)

☑ (Col-Shd Blends [1] > 0) or (S [7] > 2)

☑ (3r + (2)/R [0.32] > 0.44 and Fr + rF [1] = 0) or (3r + (2)/R [0.32] < 0.33)

☑ (Afr [0.27] < 0.46) or (Blends [13] < 4)

☑ (SumShading [10] > FM + m [6]) or (SumC' [3] > 2)

☑ (MOR [9] > 2) or (2xAB + Art + Ay [18] > 3)

CDI (Coping Deficit Index)

☐ Positive if 4 or more conditions are true:

☐ (EA [17.5] < 6) or (AdjD [2] < 0)

☐ (COP [0] < 2) and (AG [3] < 2)

☑ (Weighted Sum C [5.5] < 2.5) or (Afr [0.27] < 0.46)

☐ (Passive [9] > Active + 1 [10]) or (Pure H [3] < 2)

☑ (SumT [1] > 1) or (Isolate/R [0.47] > 0.24) or (Food [0] > 0)

2　Total

Table 8.2 continued

DEPI (Depression Index)	CDI (Coping Deficit Index)
☑ (COP [0] < 2) *or* ([Bt+2xC1+Ge+Ls + 2xNa]/R [0.47] > 0.24)	
7 Total	

HVI (Hypervigilance Index)	OBS (Obsessive Style Index)
☐ Positive if condition 1 is true and at least 4 of the others are true:	☐ (1) Dd [0] > 3
☐ (1) FT + TF + T [1] = 0	☑ (2) Zf [19] > 12
☑ (2) Zf [19] > 12	☑ (3) Zd [14.0] > +3.0
☑ (3) Zd [14.0] > +3.5	☐ (4) Populars [3] > 7
☑ (4) S [7] > 3	☐ (5) FQ+ [1] > 1
☑ (5) H + (H) + Hd + (Hd) [9] > 6	☐ Positive if one or more is true:
☐ (6) (H) + (A) + (Hd) + (Ad) [2] > 3	☐ Conditions 1 to 5 are all true
☑ (7) H + A : Hd + Ad [12:6] < 4 : 1	☐ Two or more of 1 to 4 are true *and* FQ+ [1] > 3
☐ (8) Cg [2] > 3	☐ 3 or more of 1 to 5 are true *and* X+% [0.21] > 0.89
	☐ FQ+ [1] > 3 *and* X+% [0.21] > 0.89

Note: "*" indicates a cutoff that has been adjusted for age norms.

Protocol was scored by N. Kaser-Boyd and D. Viglione, Ph.D.

Table 8.3   Structural Summary, Maria

Client Name:	Gender -Not specified-	Test Date: 02/07/1992
Client ID:	Date of Birth: 05/28/1951	Description:

Location Features

Zf	=	19
ZSum	=	77.0
Zest	=	63.0
W	=	19
(Wv	=	0)
D	=	0
Dd	=	0
S	=	7

DQ

			(FQ−)
+	=	14	(9)
o	=	4	(1)
v/+	=	1	(1)
v	=	0	(0)

Form Quality

		FQx	FQf	MQual	SQx
+	=	1	0	0	1
o	=	3	1	1	0
u	=	4	0	2	1
−	=	11	0	9	5
none	=	0	—	0	0

Determinants

Blends	Single
M.m.FC.FV	M = 2
M.CF	FM= 1
M.CF	m = 1
M.CF	FC = 0
M.YF	CF = 0
YF.C'F	C = 0
FY.FC'	Cn = 0
M.FT	FC'= 0
M.FC'.FY	C'F= 0
FM.Fr	C' = 0
M.CF	FT = 0
M.m	TF = 0
M.m.CF	T = 0
	FV= 1
	VF= 0
	V = 0
	FY= 0
	YF= 0
	Y = 0
	Fr = 0
	rF = 0
	FD= 0
	F = 1
	(2) = 3

Contents

H	= 3,0
(H)	= 1,0
Hd	= 5,0
(Hd)	= 0,0
A	= 5,2
(A)	= 1,0
Ad	= 1,0
(Ad)	= 0,0
An	= 0,1
Art	= 0,2
Ay	= 0,2
Bl	= 0,3
Bt	= 0,1
Cg	= 1,1
Cl	= 1,0
Ex	= 0,2
Fd	= 0,0
Fi	= 0,1
Ge	= 0,0
Hh	= 0,0
Ls	= 0,0
Na	= 0,3
Sc	= 0,0
Sx	= 0,2
Xy	= 0,1
Idio	= 0,0

Table 8.3 continued

S-Constellation
❑ FV+VF+ V+FD > 2
☑ Col-Shd Blends > 0
❑ Ego < .31 or > .44
☑ MOR > 3
☑ Zd > ±3.5
❑ es > EA
☑ CF + C > FC
☑ X+% < .70
☑ S > 3
❑ P < 3 or > 8
❑ Pure H < 2
❑ R < 17
6 Total

Special Scores		
	Lvl-1	Lvl-2
DV =	2 x1	0 x2
INC =	2 x2	0 x4
DR =	1 x3	4 x6
FAB =	0 x4	3 x7
ALOG =	0 x5	
CON =	0 x7	
Raw Sum6 = 12		
Wgtd Sum6 = 54		
AB = 7	CP = 1	
AG = 3	MOR= 9	
CFB = 0	PER = 1	
COP= 0	PSV = 0	

Ratios, Percentages, and Derivations

R = 19	L = 0.06
EB = 12 : 5.5	EA = 17.5
EBPer = 2.2	eb = 6 : 10
es = 16	D = 0
Adj es = 10	Adj D = +2
FM = 2	C' = 3
T = 1	m = 4
V = 2	Y = 4

Affect
FC:CF + C = 1 : 5
Pure C = 0
SumC' : WSumC = 3:5.5
Afr = 0.27
S = 7
Blends:R = 13 : 19
CP = 1

Table 8.3   continued

Interpersonal	Self-Perception	Mediation
COP = 0	3r+(2)/R = 0.32	P = 3
AG = 3	Fr+rF = 1	X+% = 0.21
Food = 0	FD = 0	F+% = 1.00
Isolate/R = 0.47	An+Xy = 2	X–% = 0.58
H : (H)+Hd+(Hd) = 3 : 6	MOR = 9	S–% = 0.45
(H)+(Hd):(A)+(Ad) = 1:1		Xu% = 0.21
H+A : Hd+Ad = 12 : 6		

Ideation		Processing
a:p = 9 : 9	Sum6 = 12	Zf = 19
Ma:Mp = 6 : 6	Lvl-2 = 7	Zd = +14.0
2AB+(Art+Ay) = 18	WSum6 = 54	W : D : Dd = 19 : 0 : 0
M– = 9	M none = 0	W : M = 19 : 12
		DQ+ = 14
		DQv = 0

☑ SCZI = 6 ☑ DEPI = 7 ❑ CDI = 2 ❑ S-CON = 6 ❑ HVI = No ❑ OBS = No

selected. Exner's Cluster and Search Strategy (Rapid Reference 8.1) provides domains and the variables that offer data for those domains. RIAP-4 automatically searches to determine which variable cluster is "key" for the protocol.

In Maria's case, the RIAP-4 program focused on variables that suggest acute distress as well as thought disorder, because DEPI was elevated and so was SCZI. The most important data to discuss, therefore, surround thought disorder and the expression of emotion or emotional dyscontrol. As noted in Chapter 5, crucial clinical determination is whether the examinee is currently suicidal. She *has* been suicidal in the past. The Rorschach scores here are a supplement to the clinical evaluation of suicidal ideation and intent, and may be especially useful for patients who seem unable or unwilling to communicate the degree of their emotional pain.

For brevity's sake, all of the variables in the Ideation, Mediation, and Processing cluster are discussed more briefly, after an examination of the examinee's affect, because it appears that she has an affective disorder and the variables surrounding affect will be the most useful in understanding the referral questions.

The examinee is positive on 6

Rapid Reference 8.1

Interpretive Search Strategy for Examinee

- Ideation, Mediation, Processing
- Controls
- Situational Stress
- Affect
- Self-Perception
- Interpersonal Perception

variables of the Suicide Constellation, including Color-Shading Blends > 0, Morbids > 3, ZD > 3.5, CF+C > FC, X+% < .70, and S > 3. Although the cutting score for significance is 8, important aspects of Maria's functioning are revealed by examining variables in the Suicide Constellation, and Exner cautions that some of the effected suicides in his research sample had fewer than 8 variables. The Suicide Constellation was empirically derived by analyzing the Rorschach scores of patients who committed suicide within 60 days after taking the Rorschach. Exner (1978) compared this data to the Rorschachs of patients who attempted suicide, as well as to control groups of those who were depressed but not suicidal. See Chapter 7 for a more detailed discussion of this research. Color-Shading Blends are found among people who have a mix of painful feelings. They may feel two or more ways about a person or an event, both of which are painful. Ambivalent, approach-avoidant, or conflicted are other ways to describe these individuals. Examinee's Rorschach *content* also exhibits this dynamic; for example, her response to Card IX: "This reminds me of my bulimia, bent over and vomiting . . . and no matter which way she turns she can't seem to control what's going on inside of her. You can see her insides here . . . they look pretty worn out."

Morbids are obtained from percepts that are "dead, damaged, or destroyed." The blots themselves do not call out morbid responses in the typical subject, and the percept of something morbid is therefore a projection. These are empirically more common in depressed individuals or those with a highly pessimistic worldview. The Morbid score is also empirically associated with an impaired sense of self, that is, the "self" feels "dead, damaged, destroyed."

Zd > 3.5 is found in individuals who make painstaking efforts to organize their worlds. They are called "overincorporators" and they may be obsessive or perfectionistic, or make extraordinary efforts to make disparate perceptions "fit together," often at the expense of good reality-testing. The examinee has a Zd of +14.0.

X+% <.70 is found in those whose reality testing is impaired. Typically this impairment is a result of too much "projection" in the process of Rorschach responding, which decreases perceptual accuracy. In real-life situations, these individuals are susceptible to distorting reality. Misperception leads to behavior that is often quite inappropriate. Such a person might completely misperceive an interaction with another person, experiencing profound rejection or threat where there is none.

The CF + C > FC and S > 3 have to do with affect (emotion). At this level, they suggest a person who experiences intense emotions, including anger, and these emotions may not be modulated by thought or other typical forms of emotional modulation. The Depression Index contains some of the same variables as S-Con. One it adds is variable COP < 2. Maria has no response scored COP. Similar individuals do not expect to experience positive human relationships.

There is more to be said about the examinee's affect. Her Lambda is .06 and her Affective Ratio is .27. The average Lambda score is between .59 and .94; in contrast, Maria's Lambda is quite low and suggests that almost every response includes a score associated with affect. She could be described as affectively labile. Her Affective Ratio of .27 is in the range of a person who attempts to withdraw from affective stimulation. Often withdrawal is the person's only strategy for coping with intense emotion and when it fails, they are overwhelmed by affective stimulation. Examinee's FC:CF + C ratio is 2:5. Responses that are scored FC have more form than color. The person who responds with a percept that has form but where color is secondary is a person who is relatively well-grounded in factual or realistic things while still responding to emotion. In contrast, the person who gives CF or C responses may be more impressionistic, more affected by color, and less able to be logical when emotion is stimulated. If this ratio is weighted to the CF + C side, it is possible that when affect is experienced, there is some sacrifice of reality-testing or judgment may be compromised by affect. Maria has the unusual score of Color Projection, which is associated with denial of unpleasant emotion and the substitution of falsely positive emotion. This is the expression of a defense mechanism and is often seen in individuals who are somewhat "hysterical" in personality organization. The examinee's Rorschach record also exhibits a variety of other emotions (expressed through Rorschach shading scores). She has two Vista responses. The empirical correlates for Vista involve painful introspection. While this is likely to intensify her depression, the Vista score is associated with better prognosis in therapy.

Revisiting the Space score, Maria has 7 Space responses. The norm for Space for depressed inpatients is 2.51 and the standard deviation is 2.30. S has been associated empirically with an oppositional, angry stance. Individuals with similar scores might have a "negative, somewhat angry attitude toward the environment," (RIAP-4, 1999) which might be chronic. Although anger may not necessarily manifest directly in overt behavior, the possibility for its eruption is there and is enhanced by the fact that the examinee's controls over emotion are not presently adequate.

When analyzing emotion, its expression, and modulation, the number of Blends is also important. The examinee has 13 Blends, while the average adult has 3, and depressed inpatients have 4.5. Certainly, she experiences her world in a complex and emotionally driven way. She has one color-shading blend. A typical interpretive statement that comes from the Color-Shading Blends is, "She is often confused by emotion and may frequently experience both positive and negative feelings in response to the same stimulus. People such as this often experience feelings more intensely than others and sometimes have more difficulty in bringing emotional situations to closure"(RIAP-4). The examinee also has Blends that contain both passive and active movement, which suggests confusion about her role and a mixed or ambivalent coping style (i.e., sometimes passive, sometimes active).

A paragraph culled from the affective variables might say, "This person gives evidence of significant affective disturbance that is likely to be associated either with Major Depressive Disorder or with a chronic dispostion to becoming depressed. The possibility should also be considered that the test findings are reflecting a depressive phase of Bipolar or Cydothymic Disorder" (RIAP-4, 1999).

So far, we have closely examined Maria's affect. What adds to concerns about this patient is the manner in which she processes reality. It should be obvious from reading this protocol that the examinee distorts reality, but her formal scores are, in fact, found in patients who have very impaired reality testing. Variables associated with reality testing and logical thought are F+, Fu, and F–%; X+, Xu, and X–%; Mu and M–%; and, in particular, the Special Scores of INC, FAB, and ALOG. Even children can achieve F+ and X+ scores of .70. This information helps to put in perspective the examinee's F+% of .00 and X+% of .11. Maria almost never responded to the inkblots in a simple, reality-based way. Only two of her responses are pure Form responses, and even these have somewhat poor Form Quality. She sees only three of the so-called popular percepts, while the average adult sees six. She may be said to have difficulty seeing the world as others do, and may therefore have difficulty responding in conventional ways. There is particular distortion surrounding human interaction. Of her 10 Human Movement responses, seven are scored "minus" and the remainder are scored "unusual." Exner (1993) has considered even the presence of one M– in the record to be troubling, suggesting unrealistic ways of viewing others. At increasing levels of M–, there is an entrenched capacity to project internal conflicts and to see others in highly unrealistic ways. These people project motives onto others which aren't there, and an analysis of the content of these responses often yields a clear picture of essential conflicts and distortions. In Maria's case, we note that her humans are often symbiotically intertwined, so much so that an "explosion" or other catastrophe was necessary to "tear them apart." This perception seems a very clear synopsis/description of her criminal offense: she states she went to her ex-boyfriend's apartment to convince him to leave her alone, and she took a bat with her in case she needed to protect herself. In reality, her assault guaranteed that they could never be together again, because a condition of her probation was that she not come near him.

When the Special Scores are examined, the most frequent, and therefore the most important, is Abstract, and Maria responded with abstract, symbolic content in seven responses. This score is associated with overly symbolic thinking and usually is associated with projection and thought disorder. Examinee seems to vacillate between highly idealized and profoundly negative abstract content (e.g, peaceful, . . . versus evil, attacking). This thinking is sometimes referred to as splitting and reflects an "all good" or "all bad" approach to the world. A person who responds to the Rorschach cards in this way often has a hypervigilant stance to the world. They see neutral stimuli as potentially threatening. Sometimes they attempt to avoid acknowledging that they see something frightening through the use of denial, and this results in a highly idealized percept. RIAP and ROR-SCAN Interpretive Reports contain many other hypotheses, but most referral questions call for a focused look at the Interpretive clusters.

The Report

A report on Rorschach results can be long and detailed or quite brief and focused on narrow questions. Many referral sources will not have the training or motivation to sort through the many possible statements that a Rorschach interpretation can generate. As a general rule, if the report is directed for use by another psychologist, the report should be detailed and include raw scores and constellations. Many of the statements in the report could be close to what is found in the RIAP-4 or ROR-SCAN interpretive report. See Appendix 6 for an example of a ROR-SCAN Scoring Summary and Sequence of Scores. Take care, however, not to simply "lift" the summary from the RIAP-4 report as it may not accurately describe the results. If the report is for an allied medical professional, a briefer report, but one that uses the language of the mental health field (e.g., terms like *splitting*) is appropriate. If the report is for the school, the Court, an employment setting, or similar referral source, a very simple description of reality testing, coping resources, and affective expression and modulation is preferable.

A psychological report can vary in organization, depending on the use to which the report will be put, the needs of the referral source, and other conditions that vary across different assessment situations. There are several key elements of a report, however. These include identifying information (including date of the assessment procedures), referral questions, behavioral observations, raw test data (especially when writing for other psychologists), a statement about validity, interpretive statements tied to test data, integration with other psychological tests, and summary and answers to the referral question(s) (see Don't Forget 8.1). Common errors in writing psychological reports include omitting the testing date or dates (psychological state can vary from time to time), providing test data that is complicated and hard to follow, failing to tie test results to normative data or data on other patient groups, and providing answers to the referral question that are too brief.

Following are examples of a report for another psychologist, written as if the referral question surrounded treatment, and a report for the Court, answering questions about dangerousness. For the sake of brevity, the following examples

DON'T FORGET 8.1

Pertinent Information for Reports

- Identifying information
- Referral question(s)
- Behavioral observations
- Life history (includes medical history, arrest history, or other specific history that is pertinent to the referral question)
- Raw test data (for reports to other psychologists)
- Statement about validity of findings
- Interpretive statements tied to test data and comparison to norms
- Integration with findings from other tests
- Summary and answers to referral questions

exclude some of the portions of a typical report, such as identifying information, life history, and referral question.

Report to Another Psychologist

Appearance and Behavior. Maria appears as a pretty, petite, blond woman. Although she is 40, she appears much younger than her age. At the time of the assessment, she was incarcerated at the women's jail, and her grooming and hygiene appeared good. The examinee cried often through the multiple-day evaluation, and she often seemed quite fearful. It was noted that she was still specifically fearful of her ex-boyfriend. She had been seen by jail medical staff, but was not prescribed any medication. The Examinee seemed well above average in intelligence, was very verbal, with an extensive vocabulary, especially about emotions.

Rorschach Results. The examinee's Rorschach provides additional rich detail that helps us to understand the nature of her unique mental state. Her Rorschach is filled with images of injury and threat. For example, to Card II, the examinee responds, "It looks like a ballet dancer, a large ballet dancer . . . these look like her feet . . . she's on her toes and this is her torso. I don't know why it (the body) would be open in the middle. It may be some sort of emblem, hanging on a chain. Maybe her body is not present, just the pieces she wears, almost as if on a hanger. [You said it looks like her body is open in the middle?] I see it both ways (as a costume with a medallion and as a woman ripped apart with her heart torn out, and blood all over her clothes. I see it both ways, but it scares me this other way, so I said clothing on a hanger." In addition to the threat to body integrity, the examinee's responses reflect the way she experiences herself and others. For example, to Card III, Examinee responds, "It looks like two people holding on to something and looks like their hearts have been torn out of their bodies, but they are connected . . . just like they are trying to pull away. Is this supposed to make me feel like this? [Beginning to cry, very upset]. I feel very scared. I just see a lot of ugliness. Looks like two people pulling, almost like they are attached to something and can't get away, pulling and pulling, too tightly connected, almost looks like attached at the top, but an explosion tore them apart, but their hearts are still connected, and are out here. I keep wanting to say this is matter, like their minds have been hurt, too, and also looks like blood behind their heads."

The people "pulling" and "too tightly connected" who need an "explosion" to tear them apart sound very much like the examinee and her boyfriend and help to explain her thinking at the time of the offense. This same type of response is repeated several times in the Rorschach record (for example, on Card VII, where she sees "Two children at odds with one another. They are the same, but they're not the same. They are attached but it's not comfortable. They are struggling to get apart. There is great torment and a lot of decay and death. [What makes it look like that?] The fact that it is all black and their mouths have all different levels of it, and everything is distorted, smudged, and smeared and not clear. Looks like children, but so old and worn out.")

Examinee's emotional turmoil or in Exner Comprehensive language, her "mix of painful feelings" is evident in her response to Card IX: "Oh, this reminds me of my bulimia. Reminds me of someone bent over and vomiting and no matter which way she turns, she can't seem to control what's going on inside of her. You can see her insides here . . . they look pretty worn out. She is back to back, as if everywhere she turns, and no matter what she did, it didn't matter, the same things would happen. This one almost looks angry, but this one just looks sad, in anguish, desperate, completely out of control, and the other one looks angry, she is throwing up her anger."

The Examinee's Rorschach record is valid and interpretively useful. Her Lambda of .06 is considerably outside of the normal range and suggests she is very affected by affective stimuli and probably emotionally labile. At the time of this Rorschach administration, examinee was quite depressed and she had a number of the variables associated with suicide risk (including Color-Shading

Blends, Morbids, CF + C > FC, poor reality testing and the DEPI is elevated). She sometimes seems to substitute a false positive emotion to a situation. Examinee seems to attempt to withdraw from affective stimulation, but when she is unable to do so, her considerable fear of injury and her painful emotions break through. She demonstrates a recently developed sense of guilt, shame, or remorse. Examinee has an unusually high number of Space responses, which indicates that anger is an important part of her mix of painful feelings. Examinee's scores in the affective domains are frequently associated with chronic and serious affective disorders.

Examinee's thinking is overly complex (number of Blends). She has an overincorporative cognitive style, which takes considerable effort but may not result in perceptual accuracy. Examinee distorts reality ($X+\% = .21$, $X-\% = .58$; $M-\% = .75$. She seems to have difficulty seeing the world as others do (Pop = 3) and may therefore have difficulty responding in conventional ways. People with similar difficulties with perceptual accuracy and translation (mediation) may be quite disorganized or inconsistent in their decision making and may have flawed judgment. At the same time, examinee appears to have considerable resources with which to form and implement decisions. Her current cognitive and emotional disarray may stem from the experience of an increase in stimulus demands, perhaps because her current level of stress is severe. Her excellent cognitive resources can be employed in therapy to assist her with the modulation of her affect and to learn better coping skills.

There is particular distortion surrounding human interaction. Of her 10 Human Movement responses, 7 are scored "minus" and the remainder are scored "unusual." This will certainly influence the manner in which she perceives and relates to others. Examinee's thinking often becomes overly abstract and symbolic, and at these times her thinking seems minimally constrained by logic. Examinee is also elevated on SCZI. While this score has been associated with schizophrenia, it should be considered a general index of thought disorder and combined with the history and course of symptoms. In examinee's case, there is no history of schizoprehenic symptoms. Instead, the history reveals multiple traumas that contained the threat of serious injury or death, and her current affective disarray and thought disorder seem clearly tied to fears of injury and threat.

Examinee's self-representations are also affected by her tendency to distort her perceptions. While she appears to be quite self-involved, this takes the form of rumination about characteristics she feels are very undesireable. She appears to be preoccupied with body integrity, a finding often seen in individuals who feel very vulnerable.

Integration with Other Tests. MMPI-2 results suggest a person in significant distress, who is likely not "faking" or exaggerating. She exhibits marked elevations on Scales 3, 2, and 1, in that order. A Scale 3 elevation at this level ($T = 94$) is found in individuals with the capacity for hysterical dissociative episodes, usually brought on by extreme stress. These individuals often have an early history of abuse or trauma. They have very strong needs for attention and approval, and often their crises are precipitated by interpersonal loss or rejection. Scale 8 is not elevated, but Scale 6 is $T = 74$, revealing a clear risk of impaired reality testing, especially surrounding human relationships. Examinee also has many features of a person with a Major Affective Disorder (Scale 2 = 88) and she has a number of somatic concerns (Scale 1 = T82) similar to those found in patients with chronic pain, complicated by psychological factors. Examinee's K Scale ($T = 37$) additionally suggests she is presently profoundly vulnerable, with very low self-esteem and poor boundaries.

On the MCMI-III, examinee is significantly elevated on the Personality Pattern Scales of Avoidant, Dependent, and Self-Defeating. This is a common triad in women who have been in abusive relationships. Dependent women are gullible and easily manipuated. They feel anxiously helpless when not in a relationship with a strong significant "other." Individuals who are Avoidant have strong approach-avoidance conflicts toward others; they want to be close and trusting, but they anticipate harm, possibly because of past harm. Individuals with similar scores on Self-Defeating tend to relate to others in a self-sacrificing, servile manner and seem to accept undeserved blame and allow others to exploit or take advantage. They frequently experience deeply conflicting feelings about themselves and others, most notably, love, rage, and guilt. Their psychological "self" has a dual quality, with conflicting needs and motives, resulting in actions that may be self-sabotaging. Examinee is also significantly elevated on the Clinical Syndrome scales Major Depression and Dysthymia.

Summary and Recommendations. This woman should be considered for immediate crisis intervention. Her suicidal ideation and possible plan should be assessed. A multidisciplinary approach is likely to be more useful than psychotherapy alone. Examinee's M– tendency will likely influence her response to caregivers, requiring some time to build trust. The most immediate goal of treatment is to help examinee regain a sense of safety and gain better control over turbulent affects of anxiety and anger. Long-term treatment is likely to be necessary and should ultimately span a number of domains, including images of self and others, coping skills, management of depressed and fearful affect, and decreasing self-defeating behavior.

Report to the Court

Appearance and Behavior. Maria appears as a pretty, petite, blond woman. Although she is 40, she appears much younger than her age. At the time of the assessment, she was incarcerated at the women's jail, and her grooming and hygiene appeared good. The examinee cried often through the multiple-day evaluation, and she often seemed quite fearful. It was noted that she was still specifically fearful of her ex-boyfriend. She had been seen by jail medical staff but was not prescribed any medication. The examinee seemed well above average in intelligence, was very verbal, with an extensive vocabulary, especially about emotions. She did not make any threats about her ex-boyfriend, and she did not verbalize homicidal ideation.

Test Results. MMPI-2 results suggest a person in significant distress, who is likely not "faking" or exaggerating. This profile is found in individuals with the capacity for hysterical dissociative episodes, usually brought on by extreme stress. These individuals often have an early history of abuse or trauma. They have very strong needs for attention and approval, and often their crises are precipitated by interpersonal loss or rejection. There is a clear risk of impaired reality testing, especially surrounding human relationships. Examinee also has many features of a person with a Major Affective Disorder and she has a number of somatic concerns similar to those found in patients with chronic pain, complicated by psychological factors. Examinee is presently profoundly vulnerable, with very low self-esteem and poor boundaries.

On the MCMI-III, examinee is significantly elevated on the Personality Pattern Scales of Avoidant, Dependent, and Self-Defeating. This is a common triad in women who have been in abusive relationships. Dependent women are gullible and easily manipuated. They feel anxiously helpless when not in a relationship with a strong significant "other." Individuals who are Avoidant have strong approach-avoidance conflicts toward others; they want to be close and trusting, but they anticipate harm, possibly because of past harm. Individuals with similar scores on Self-Defeating tend to relate to others in a self-sacrificing, servile manner and seem to accept undeserved blame and allow others to exploit or take advantage. They frequently experience deeply conflicting feelings about themselves and others, most notably, love, rage, and guilt. On the Clinical Syndrome Scales, examinee's elevations suggest difficulty sleeping, feelings of hopelessness, a fear of the future, agitation, and psychomotor retardation. Other features include feeling physically drained, becoming angry or tearful with little provocation, feeling unworthy or undeserving, and significant mental confusion.

Examinee's Rorschach provides additional rich detail that helps us to understand the nature of her unique mental state. It is important to note that the Rorschach is a difficult instrument to "fake," since it is an ambiguous task and much of the material associating responses to psychopathology is in obscure journals. Examinee's Rorschach is filled with images of injury and threat and with the sense of another "self," possibly a dissociated self. In her Rorschach content, there is symbolic expression of the dynamics that led to the present offense, for example, in the response, "Two people holding on to something . . . looks like their hearts have been torn out of their bodies, but they are connected. It is like they are trying to pull away . . . two people pulling, almost like they are attached to something and can't get away, pulling and pulling, too tightly connected, almost looks like they were attached at the top but an explosion tore them apart, but their hearts are still connected." Examinee's thinking is overly complex and profoundly influenced by emotions of self-denigration, fear, threat, and anger. She does not see human relationships realistically; her perceptions are at times overly idealistic and at other times filled with morbidity and fears of harm. Examinee's scores in the affective domains are frequently associated with chronic and serious affective disorders (i.e., clinical depression, marked mood shifts). When under the sway of strong emotion, she is likely to have poor control of impulses. If she felt threatened, her reality testing and emotional control would be further impaired.

Response to the Court's Questions. This woman should be considered for immediate crisis intervention. Her suicidal ideation and possible plan should be assessed. There is no current homicidal ideation, but she should be required to participate in a treatment plan that is focused on her sense of threat from her ex-boyfriend and her tendency to see him as out to get her. She is not currently a danger to him or to others, but he should be advised not to make contact with her, and the court should impose mutual restraining orders on the parties. Long-term treatment is likely to be necessary for this woman and should ultimately span a number of domains, including images of self and others, coping skills, management of depressed and fearful affect, and decreasing self-defeating behavior.

🔖 TEST YOURSELF 🔖

1. **List four common errors that examiners typically make in report writing.**
   (a) _____
   (b) _____
   (c) _____
   (d) _____

2. **Some reasons for including every possible Rorschach score and interpretation in a report are:**
   (a) The report goes to another psychologist who is likely to be familiar with the Rorschach.
   (b) The report will be used for teaching purposes.
   (c) The report may be the subject of controversy, as in a Workman's Compensation claim or a criminal or custody court.
   (d) It will look inadequate to leave out any Rorschach data.

3. **It is all right to quote from the RIAP or ROR-SCAN Interpretive Reports.**
   (a) No, because they are copyrighted.
   (b) No, because they are meant as clinician-to-clinician statements and are meant to be synthesized with other clinical and test data.
   (c) Yes, because they are developed by psychology professionals, and are based on research.
   (d) Yes, but it is important to know the source of the interpretative statement (i.e., what score it comes from and what research), so the RIAP and ROR-SCAN hypotheses can be weighed against each other.

4. Rorschach results can be written about separately or integrated with the results of other tests. When the latter approach is taken, the general organization of the report can follow common domains of psychological functioning, such as

   (a) Reality testing.

   (b) Emotional control.

   (c) Self-concept.

   (d) Relationships with others.

   (e) all of the above.

5. A Rorschach results section could be as short as one paragraph. True or False?

Answers: 1. Report not directed to the referral question, too complicated for the typical reader, doesn't include scores on which interpretations are derived, doesn't tie conclusions to test findings; 2. a, b, and c; 3. d; 4. e; 5. True.

Appendix I
RORSCHACH RESPONSE FORM

Name/Id# _____ Date: ___ / ___ / ___

Card	Resp.#	Response	Inquiry

Appendix 2

RORSCHACH SCRIPT: INTRODUCTORY AND RESPONSE PHASE

I. Introducing the test

1. Prepare the person during the introductory overview phase of assessment.

". . . One of the tests we will be doing is the inkblot test, the Rorschach. Have you ever heard of it, or have you ever taken it?"

I'm going to show you a series of inkblots and I want you to tell me what you think they look like.

2. Why is the test used?

"It is a test that gives us some information about your personality, and by having that information we can . . . (plan your treatment easier; understand your problem a bit better; answer some of the questions you have about yourself more precisely; make some recommendations that your doctor has requested; get some idea about how your treatment program is progressing, etc.)"

3. How can you get anything out of this?

It is better to wait to answer these questions until we have finished all of the testing/our work together/the assessment.

II. Response

1. When you hand the subject a card

"What might this be?"

2. Subject's questions about what to see or if they can turn the cards, or how many responses

"Just tell me what you see there."

"It's up to you."

"Most people find more than one thing."

"People see all kinds of things."

3. If there is only 1 response to the first card

"Take your time and then look some more. I'm sure you'll find something else too."

How many should I find? "It's up to you."

4. If there is more than 5 responses to the first card

After the fifth response, take the card from the subject and say, "All right, let's do the next one." (Repeat for each successive card until 5 or fewer responses are given. Then no longer comment on subsequent blots even if over 5 responses are offered.)

5. When a subject says she/he does not see anything

"Take your time. We're in no hurry. Everyone can find something."

6. When a subject is speaking too quickly

"Wait! I'm having trouble keeping up with you. Go a little slower please."

"I'm sorry, I didn't get all of that. You said two people with hats and . . . ?"

7. Fewer than 14 responses are not accepted. If there are fewer than 14 do not go on until:

"Now you know how it's done. But there's a problem. You didn't give enough answers for us to get anything out of the test. So we will go through them again and this time I want you to make sure to give me more answers. You can include the same ones you've already given if you like but make sure to give me more answers this time."

"Well, it's really up to you, but you only gave __ answers and I really need more than that to get anything out of the test."

"Well, it's up to you but I really need several more answers than you gave."

Appendix 3

RORSCHACH SCRIPT: INQUIRY PHASE

1. Standard explanation and responses to general questions

"Now we are going to go back through the cards again. It won't take very long. I want to see the things that you said you saw, and make sure that I see them like you do. We'll do them one at a time. I'll read what you said and then I want you to show me where it is in the blot and then tell me what is there that makes it look like that so that I can see it too, just like you did. Is that clear?"

Why do we have to do this? "So that I can see the things that you saw"

What do you want me to tell you? "Just show me where you saw it and what makes it look like that."

Should I find other things too? "No, I'm only interested in the things you saw before."

If subject (still) seems unsure "Remember, I need to see it as you do. I need to know where it is and what about the blot makes it look that way."

2. Initial questions after handing the card to the subject

"Here you said . . ." or "Then you said . . ."

Yes that's right. "Remember now why we're doing this. I need to see it too, so you have to help me. Show me where it is and tell me what makes it look like that."

I don't know why, it just looks like that to me. "I know it looks like that to you but remember, I need to see it too. So help me. Tell me about some of the things you see there that make it look like ____ "

3. You want to understand

(A) *Location*: "where is it?" (Looking for: W, D, Dd, S)
(B) *Determinants*: "what makes it look like that?" (Looking for: form, movement, any color, shading, dimension, pairs/reflections)
(C) *Content*: "what is it?"

4. *Questioning*

(A) *Location questions:* "Where is it that you see that?"; "I don't think I see it correctly, run your finger around it."; "I'm not sure where it is, put your finger on the . . . (nose, wheel, etc.)." [Do this on the blot, not the location sheet.]

(B) *Determinants questions:* "I'm not sure what makes it look like that."

(C) *Basic prompt:* "I'm not sure I see it as you do, help me."; "You'll have to help me, I don't think I'm seeing it yet."; "I know it looks like that to you, but remember I have to see it too. So help me to understand why it looks like that to you."

5. *Key words to repeat*

Adjectives and movement / verbs

6. *Never ask leading questions.*

Period.

7. *Subject's resistance*

I didn't say that or I don't know, I can't see it now. "Come on now. Look, I wrote it down. you can find it, take your time." [Be firm and tactful.] "Take your time. We are in no hurry. You found it once. I'm sure you can find it again."

(From W: pp.3–22; V1: pp. 67–82)

Appendix 4

RORSCHACH SCORING WORKSHEET

Name / Id: _____   Card: _____   Response No.: _____

Directions: For each category, fill in the blank space with a score/code or check the not applicable box (☐ n/a).
Under "Why", write in the basis for your coding decision.

Index: ( ) = Special directions   { } = Scoring options for each category
[ ] = Pages in Exner's 1995 Workbook (W) and 1993 Comprehensive System: Volume 1 (V1)

1. Location and Developmental Quality (DQ)

Location: _____   {W, D, Dd, S; if D, Dd or S, look up location number} [W: 23-25; V1: 93-97]

Why: _____

Developmental Quality: _____   (Goes after Location) {+, v/+, o, v} [W: 25-28; V1: 97-101]

Why: _____

2. Determinant(s)

Form	_____	{F} [W: 33-34; V1: 106]
Movement & Active-Passive Superscripts	_____	(Movement followed by a/p superscript) {M, FM, *m*}$^{a, p, a-p}$ } [W: 34; V1: 106-109] [W: 35-36; V1: 109-113]
Chromatic Color	☐ n/a	{C, CF, FC, Cn} [W: 36-39; V1: 113-120]
Achromatic Color	☐ n/a	{C', CF, FC'} [W: 39-40; V1: 120-122]
Shading-Texture	☐ n/a	{T, TF, FT} [W: 40- 41; V1: 124-127]
Shading-Vista	☐ n/a	{V, VF, FV} [W: 41-42; V1: 127-128]

Appendix 4 continued

RORSCHACH SCORING WORKSHEET

Shading-Diffuse   ☐ n/a _____ {Y, YF, FY} [W: 42; V1: 128-133]

Form Dimension   ☐ n/a _____ {FD} [W: 42-43; V1: 131-133]

Pairs and Reflections ☐ n/a _____ {(2), rF, Fr} [W: 43; V1: 133-137]

Why: _____

3. Form Quality   ☐ n/a _____ (Goes under "Determinants and FQ" at the end of the row; select the most conservative score) {+, o, u, -}
[W: 46-51, 101-161; V1: 150-155, 153-195]
Why: _____

4. Content(s)   ☐ n/a _____ (Goes under "Content") {H, (H), Hd, (Hd), Hx, A, (A), Ad, (Ad), An, Art, Ay, Bl, Bt, Cg, Cl, Ex, Fi, Fd, Ge, Hh, Ls, Na, Sc, Sx, Xy} [W: 52-56; V1:157-160]
Why: _____

5. Popular Responses   ☐ n/a _____ (Goes under "Pop") {P} [W: 56-57; V1: 160-163]
Why: _____

6. Organizational Activity (Z-score)   ☐ n/a _____ (Goes under "Z-Score", use only if response contains: W(DQ+,v/+,o), adj. detail, distant detail or white space with detail; choose the highest score) {#} [W: 58-60; V1: 145-150]

7. Special Scores   ☐ n/a _____ (Goes under "Special Scores") {DV, DR, INCOM, FABCOM, CONTAM, ALOG, PSV, CONFAB, AG, COP, MOR, AB, PER, CP}
[W: 61-76; V1: 165-174]
Why: _____

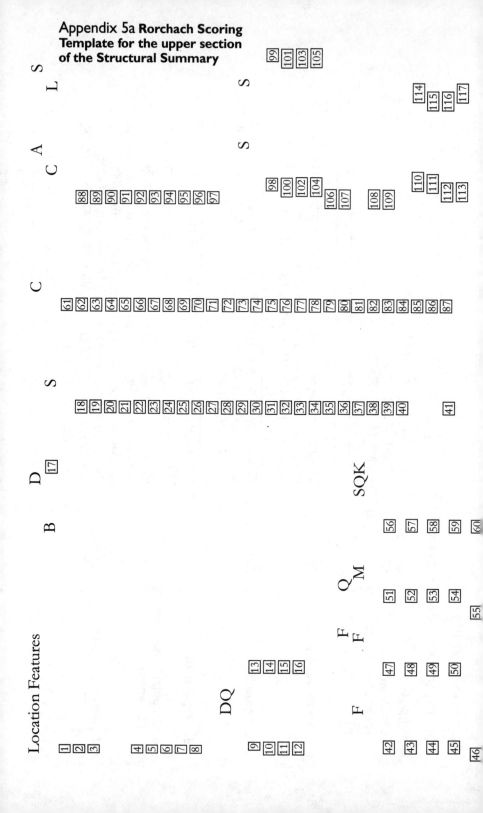

Appendix 5a **Rorchach Scoring Template for the upper section of the Structural Summary**

Location Features

Appendix 5b Rorchach Scoring Template for the lower section of the Structural Summary

R   P   A   D

Section 1

L.1.1   1.2

1.3   1.4   1.5
1.6   1.7   1.8
1.9   1.10

1.11   1.12   1.13
1.14   1.15   1.16

Section 2

L.2.1
2.2   2.5
2.3   2.6
2.4   2.7
       2.8

Section 3

L.3.1
3.2
3.3
3.4
3.5
3.6

Section 4

L.4.1
4.2
4.3
4.4
4.5
4.6

Section 5

L.5.1
5.2
5.3
5.4
5.5
5.6

Section 6

6.2

L.6.1
6.3
6.4
6.5
6.6
6.7

Section 7

L.7.1
7.2
7.3
7.4
7.5

Appendix 6

ROR-SCAN SCORING SUMMARY

Name: Maria	Sex: F	Examiner: Nancy Kaser-Boyd, Ph.D.
ID: PIWA0714.RW5 Ed: 12	Age: 41	Date Tested: 2/7/92

	Loc	W	D	Dd	S		DQ	+	o	v	v/+		FQ	+	o	u	-	no
R 19	Loc	19	0	0	7		DQ	14	4	0	1		FQx	1	3	4	11	0
	FQ-	11	0	0	5		DQ	9	1	0	1		FQf	0	1	0	0	0
L 0.06	S	7	0	0			FQ-	14	4	0	1		FQM	0	1	2	9	0
							W						FQS	1	0	1	5	0

DETERMINANTS
Single, Blend

BLENDS:R 13:19

*Ma,mp,FC,FV-	Mp,CF-
Mp,CF-	Mp,CF-
Mp,YF-	^YF,C'F-
^YF,FC'u	Ma,FT-
^Ma,FC',FYo	FMa,Fro
Ma,CF-	Mp,ma-
Ma,ma,CFu	

Pure F 1

FC	0,1		FC'	0,2		FV	1,1		FY	0,2
CF	0,5		CF'	0,1		VF	0,0		YF	0,2
C	0,0		C'	0,0		V	0,0		Y	0,0
Cn	0,0		FT	0,1						
			TF	0,0		Fr	0,1			
			T	0,0		rF	0,0			
						FD	0,0			

	a/p	
M	2,10	6/6
m	1,3	2/2
FM	1,1	1/1

COMPOSITES

EB	12:5.5 (IN)		EA	17.5
eb	6:10		es	16
			adj es	10
			D	0
			AdjD	+2

FM	2	C'	3	V	2
m	4	T	1	Y	4

Pure C	0		Ego	.32
FC:CF+C	1:5		(2)	3
Afr	.27		Fr+rF	1

X+%	21	F+%	100
Xu%	21	Pop	3
X-%	58	S-%	45

Zf	19
Zsum	77.0
Zest	63.0
Zd	+14.0

An+Xy:R	2:19
Isolate/R	0.47
2AB+Art+Ay:R	18:19
H+A:Hd+Ad	10:6
(H)+(Hd):(A)+(Ad)	1:1
H:Hd+(H)+(Hd)	3:6

Ma:Mp	6:6	W:M	19:12
a:p	9:9	W:D	19:0

Appendix 6 continued

ROR-SCAN SCORING SUMMARY

SPECIAL SCORES

	(FQ-)		level 1,2	Aggression Categories	
AB	7	(6)	DV	2,0	AgC	0
AG	3	(2)	INC	2,0	AgPot	0
CFB	0		DR	1,4	AgPast	0
COP	0		FAB	0,3	SM	0
CP	1		ALG	0		
MOR	9	(7)	CTM	0		
PER	1	(1)	Sum6	12		
PSV	0		WSum6	54		

CONTENTS

H	3	Fd	0
Hd	5	Ge	0
(H)	1	Hh	0
(Hd)	0	Id	0
Hx	5	Ls	0
A	7	Na	3
Ad	1	Sc	0
(A)	2	Sx	2
(Ad)	0	Xy	1

INDICES	
HVI	-
SCZI	+
DEPI	+
SCON	-
OBS	-
CDI	-

Scores:		
Dd>3	(a)	*
Zf>12	(b)	*
Zd>+3	(c)	
Pop>7	(d)	
FQ+>1	(e)	

INDICES (@=adjusted for age)

SCZI	
X+%<61 & S-%<41	+
or X+%<50	+
X-%>29	+
FQx->=FQxu	+
or FQ->(FQo+FQ+)	
Lvl2>1 & FAB2>0	+
@Sum6SPSC>6	+
or @WSum6SPSC>17	+
M->1 or X-%>40	-
SCZI = 6	
(pos>=4)	

HVI	
S>3	+
Zf>12	+
SumH>6	+
Zd>+3.5	+
Sum( )>3	-
H+A:Hd+Ad<4:1	+
Cg>3	-
T=1	
(if T=0, pos>=4)	
HVI = 5	
(pos>=4)	

DEPI	
SumV>0 or FD>2	+
C-S BI>0 or S>2	+
@Ego>.44 & Sumr=0	+
or @Ego<.33	
Afr<.46 or Bl<4	+
b>e or SumC'>2	+
MOR>2 or Intel>3	+
COP<2 or Iso>.24	+
DEPI = 7	
(pos>=5)	

SCON			
SumV+FD>2	-	CF+C>FC	+
C-S BI>0	+	X+%<70	+
Ego<.31>.44	-	S>3	+
or @Ego>.33		P<3>8	-
MOR>3	+	Pure H<2	-
Zd>+-3.5	+	R<17	-
es>EA	-		
SCON = 6			
(pos>=8)			

CDI	
EA<6 or AdjD<0	-
COP<2 & AG<2	-
WSumC<2.5 or Afr<.46	+
p>a+1 or PureH<2	-
T>1 or Iso>.24 or Fd>0	+
CDI = 2	
(pos>=4)	

OBS	
Conditions:	
abcde	-
abcd>2 & FQ+>3	-
abcde>3 & X+%>89	-
FQ+>3 & X+%>89	-
OBS = 0	
(pos>=1)	

Appendix 6 continued

ROR-SCAN SEQUENCE OF RESPONSES

Name:
ID: PIWA0714.RW5   **Ed:** 12

Sex: F
Age: 41

Examiner: Nancy Kaser-Boyd, Ph.D.
Date Tested: 2/7/92

Loc/DQ	#	Determinant/FQ	(2)	Content	P	Z	Special Score	Ag Categories
Card I								
1 WS+	1	FV+		Hd,Sx		4.0		
2 WSo	1	FMpu		A		3.5	MOR,INC1	
Card II								
3 WS+	1	Ma,mp,FC,FV-		A,Bl,Hx		4.5	AG,MOR,AB,DR2	
4 WS+	1	mp-		Cg,Art		4.5		
5 WS+	1	Mp,CF-		Hd,Bl		4.5	MOR	
Card III								
6 W+	1	Mp,CF-	2	H,Bl,Ex,Hx	P	5.5	MOR,AB,DR2	
7 WS+	1	Mp,CF-		Hd,Xy		5.5	MOR,FAB2	
Card IV								
8 W+	1	Mp,YF-		(H),A,Bt		4.0	AB	
9 W/	1	YF,C'F-		Cl,A,Na,Ay		4.0	AB,MOR,DR1	

Appendix 6 continued

ROR-SCAN SEQUENCE OF RESPONSES

Card V					
10 Wo	1	Fo	A	1.0	DR2
11 W+	1	Mau	(A),Cg	2.5	INC1
12 Wo	1	Mp–	Hd,Art	1.0	
Card VI					
13 Wo	1	FY,FC'u	Ad,Ay	2.5	CP
14 WS+	1	Ma,FT–	Hd,Sx	6.5	DV1
Card VII					
15 W+	1	Ma,FC',FYo	2 H,Hx	P 2.5	MOR,AG,FAB2,AB
Card VIII					
16 W+	1	FMa,Fro	A,Na	P 4.5	DR2
Card IX					
17 W+	1	Ma,CF–	H,Hx,An	5.5	MOR,AG,PER,AB
18 W+	1	Mp,ma–	Hx,Fi	5.5	AB,MOR
Card X					
19 W+	1	Ma,ma,CFu	2 A,Ex,Na	5.5	DV1,FAB2

Reproduced by special permission of Philip F. Caracena, Ph.D. Future reproduction is prohibited without permission of Philip Caracena.

References

Aronow, E., and Reznikoff, M. (1976). *Rorschach content interpretation*. New York: Grune & Stratton.

Atkinson, L. The comparative validities of the Rorschach and MMPI: A meta-analysis. *Canadian Psychology, 27,* 238–347.

Beck, S. J. 1937. *Introduction to the Rorschach Method*. New York: American Orthopsychiatric Association.

Berg, J., Gacano, C., Meloy, J. R., and Pesslee, J. (1994). "A Rorschach comparison of borderline and antisocial females." Unpublished manuscript.

Binet, A. and Henri,V. (1895–96). La psychologie individuelle, *La Annee Psychologique, 2,* 411–465.

Butcher, J. N., & Rouse, S.V. (1966). Personality: Individual differences and clinical assessment. *Annual Review of Psychology, 47,* 87–111.

Dearborn, G.V. (1897). Blots of ink in experimental psychology. *Psychological Review, 4,* 390–391.

Dearborn, G.V. (1898). A study of imaginations. *American Journal of Psychology, 9,* 183–190.

DeVoss, G. & Boyer, L. B. (1989). *Symbolic analysis cross-culturally: the Rorschach test.* Berkeley, CA: University of California Press.

Ellenberger, H. (1954). The life and work of Hermann Rorschach (1884–1922). *Bulletin of the Minninger Clinic, 18,* 173–219.

Exner, J. E. (1974). *The Rorschach: A comprehensive system: Volume 1: Basic foundations,* New York: Wiley.

Exner, J. E. & Bryant, E. L. (1974). Rorschach responses of subjects recently divorced or separated. Workshops Study No. 206 (unpublished). Rorschach workshops.

Exner, J. E. (1978). The Rorschach: A comprehensive system, Volume 2. Recent research and advanced interpretation. New York: Wiley.

Exner, J. E. (1991). *The Rorschach: A comprehensive system: Volume 2: 2 Interpretations* (2nd ed.). New York: Wiley.

Exner, J. E. (1993). *The Rorschach: A comprehensive system: Volume 1: Basic Foundations* (3rd ed.). New York: Wiley.

Exner, J. E. & Weiner, I. (1994). *The Rorschach: A comprehensive system: Volume 3: Assessment of children and adolescents* (2nd ed.). New York: Wiley.

Exner, J. E. (1995). *A Rorschach workbook for the comprehensive system* (4th ed.). Asheville, NC: Rorschach Workshops.

Exner, J. E. (1996). A comment on "The Comprehensive System for the Rorschach: A Critical Examination." *Psychological Science, 7,* 11–13.

Frank, L. K. (1939). Projective methods for the study of personality. *Journal of Psychology, 8,* 389–413.

Gacano, C. & Meloy, J. R. (1994). *The Rorschach assessment of aggressive and psychopathic personalities.* Hillsdale, NJ; Lawrence Erlbaum Associates.

Gacano, C. B., Meloy, J. R., & Berg J. L. (1992). Object relations, defensive operations, and affective states in narcissistic, borderline and antisocial personality disorder. *Journal of Personality Assessment, 59,* 32–47.

Graham, J. R. (1990). *MMPI-2: Assessing personality and psychopathology.* New York: Oxford Univeristy Press.

Hertz, M. R. The Reliability of the Rorschach inkblot test. *Journal of Applied Psychology, 18,* 461–77.

Hertz, M. R. (1936). The method of administration of the Rorschach Inkblot Test, *Child Development, 7,* 237–54.

Hilsenroth, M. J., Handler, L., Toman, K. M., and Padawer, J. R. (1995). Rorschach and MMPI-2 indices of early psychotherapy termination. *Journal of Consulting & Clinical Psychology, 63(6),* 956–965.

Kaser-Boyd, N. (1993). Rorschachs of women who commit homicide. *Journal of Personality Assessment 60(3),* 458–470.

Kaser-Boyd, N. (1999). The forensic evaluation of PTSD. Workshop at the Society for Personality Assessment Annual Meeting, New Orleans, LA.

Kerner, J. (1857). *Kleksographien.* Tubingen, Germany.

Kirkpatrick, E. A. (1900). Individual tests of school children. *Psychological Review, 7,* 274–80.

Klopfer, B. (1937). The present status of the theoretical development of the Rorschach Method. *Rorschach Research Exchange, 1,* 142–47.

Klopfer, B. and Davidson, H. H. (1962). *The Rorschach technique: An introductory manual.* New York: Harcourt Brace Jovanovich.

Krall V., Sachs H., Lazar B., Rayson R., Growe G., Novar, L., & O'Connell, L. (1983). Rorschach norms for inner-city children. *Journal of Personality Assessment, 44,* 2.

Lcura, A. V. and Exner, J. E. (1976). Rorschach performances of children with a multiple foster home history. Workshops Study No. 220 (unpublished), Rorschach Workshops.

Lerner, P. M. & Lerner, H. (1980). Rorschach assessment of primitive defenses in borderline personality structure. In J. Kwawer, H. Lerner, P. Lerner, & A. Sugarman (Eds.) *Borderline pheomena and the Rorschach test* (pp. 257–274). New York: International Universities Press.

Meloy, J. R., Gacono, C. B, and Kenney, L. (1994). A Rorschach investigation of sexual homicide. *Journal of Personality Assessment,* 62(I), 58–67.

Nash, M. R., Hulsey, T. L. & Lambert, W. (1993). Long-term sequelae of childhood sexual abuse: Perceived family environment, psychopathology, and dissociation. *Journal of Consulting and Clinical Psychology, 62*(2), 276–283.

Parker, K. C., Hanson, R. K., & Hunsley, J. (1988). MMPI, Rorschach and WAIS: A meta-analytic comparison of reliability, stability and validity. *Psychological Bulletin, 103,* 367–373.

Parsons, C. J. (1917). Children's interpretations of inkblots, *British Journal of Psychology, 9,* 74–92.

Piotrowski, C. & Keller, J. W. (1984). Psychodiagnostic testing in APA-approved clinical psychology programs. *Professional Psychology, 15,* 450–456.

Piotrowski, Z. A. (1957). *Perceptanalysis.* New York: Macmillan.

Rapaport, D., Gill, M. & Schafer, R. (1946). *Diagnostic psychological testing* (vol. 2). Chicago, IL: Year Book Publishers.

Reichlin, R. E. (1984). Current perspectives on Rorschach performance among older adults. *Journal of Personality Assessment, 48* (1), 453–458.

Rorschach, H. (1921). *Psychodiagnostics.* Bern, Switzerland: Bircher.

Sachs, J. and Lee, H. B. (1992). Dual scaling analysis of Rorschach responses in a Hong Kong Chinese Sample. *Psychologia: An International Journal of Psychology in the Orient,* 35(2), 84–95.

Viglione (1980). A study of the effect of stress and state anxiety on Rorschach performance. Doctoral dissertation. Long Island University.

Watkins, C. E., Jr., Campbell, V. L., Nieberding, R., & Hallmark, R. (1995). Contemporary practice of psychological assessment by clinical psychologists. *Professional Psychology, 26,* 54–60.

Weber, A. (1937). Delirium tremens and alkoholhalluzinose in Rorschachschen Formdeutversuch. Zeitschrift fur die gesamte Neurologie und Psychiatrie, 159.

Weiner, I. B. (1996). Some Observations on the validity of the Rorschach Inkblot Method. *Psychological Assessment, 8(2),* 206–213.

Weiner, I. B. (1997). Current status of the Rorschach Inkblot Method, *Journal of Personality Assessment, 68(1),* 5–19.

Weiner, I. B. (1998). *Principles of Rorschach interpretation.* Mahwah, N.J.: Erlbaum Associates.

Weiner, I. B. & Exner, J.E. (1991). Rorschach changes in long-term and short-term psychotherapy. *Journal of Personality Assessment, 56,* 453–465.

Whipple, G. M. (1910). *Manual of mental and physical tests.* Baltimore, MD: Warwick and York.

Annotated Bibliography

Archer, R. P. (Ed.)(1999). Special series on perspectives on the Rorschach. *Assessment, 6.*
The entire journal issue is devoted to a debate on the Rorschach. Like the Meyer reference below, the most vocal critics of the Rorschach and published researchers on the Rorschach were invited to present their views. Included in this issue are articles by Garb ("Call for a Moratorium on the use of the Rorschach"); Wood and Lilienfeld ("The Rorschach Inkblot Test: A case of overstatement?"); Acklin ("Behavioral science foundations of the Rorschach test"); and Weiner ("What the Rorschach can do for you: Incremental validity in clinical applications").

DeVos, G. A., & Boyer, L. B. (1989). *Symbolic analysis cross-culturally.* Berkeley: University of California Press.
There are few current texts that provide information about the Rorschach in non-American samples. Although DeVos and Boyer's research was conducted before the wide use of the Exner Comprehensive System, their work begins the understanding of the cross-cultural utility of the Rorschach. DeVoss and Boyer are anthropologists and they argue that "personality" and "psychopathology" are not different in other cultures. They present research with samples from Japan and Algeria. The book also has three chapters on Native Americans. Although these data can't be used as contemporary norms for these groups, the material begins to illustrate how other cultures differ in 'personality traits' and how they are the same.

Exner, J. E. (Ed.). (1995). *Issues and methods in Rorschach research.* Mahwah, NJ: Lawrence Erlbaum Associates.
This is a fundamental text for anyone planning a Rorschach research study. The book contains chapters on conceptual issues, variable selection, issues in subject selection and design, statistical power in Rorschach research, and basic issues in data analysis.

Exner, J. E. (1993). *The Rorschach: A comprehensive system Volume 1: Basic foundations,* third edition. New York: John Wiley & Sons.
Primary source for all Rorschach scoring and interpretation. Exner presents the principles of administration, scoring, and interpretation. An absolute necessity if administering the Rorschach. We suggest indexing the book with post-its as you read it in order to help reference the material later.

Exner, J. E. (1994). *A Rorschach workbook for the Comprehensive System* (4th Edition). Asheville, NC: Rorschach Workshops.
The most useful reference guide when scoring the Rorschach and tabulating the scores. The workbook contains Table A, with form quality information for thousands of Rorschach responses, and formulas for calculating the ratios and summary scores by hand. Scoring rules are explained and practice responses are included in the appendix.

Exner, J. E. (1991). *The Rorschach: A comprehensive system, Volume 2, Current research and advanced interpretation,* Second edition. New York: John Wiley.
Summarizes research completed between 1973 and 1990, and covers over 300 studies. Exner presents the major interpretive postulates for using the Rorschach, covering structural assessment, content assessment, diagnosis and prediction, simulation, and malingering.

Exner, J. E. (1995). *The Rorschach: A comprehensive system, Volume 3: Assessment of children and adolescents,* Second edition. New York: John Wiley & Sons.

This book provides the information needed to interpret the younger client's Rorschach. Describes the usefulness of the Rorschach with children and adolescents, as well as basic foundational tools. Includes revised normative data from children ages 5 to 16 years old. Case studies are included throughout the book. A necessity if you are administering the Rorschach to children and/or adolescents.

Gacono, C. B., & Meloy, J. R. (1994). *The Rorschach assessment of aggressive and psychopathic personalities.* Lawrence Erlbaum Associates.

This book focuses on the study of antisocial character pathology and its assessment with the Rorschach. Clinical data from hospitals and prisons are used to describe violent and antisocial individuals. The data are analyzed using Exner's Comprehensive System, as well as psychoanalytic and developmental approaches.

Ganellen, R. (Ed.) (1996). Special series: Integrating the Rorschach and MMPI-2: Adding apples and oranges. *Journal of Personality Assessment,* 67(3). 558–587.

Ganellen and other commentators (Robert Archer, David Nichols, Steve Finn, Greg Meyer, and Dan Viglione) note and explain the frequently cited absence of correspondence in MMPI-2 and Rorschach results and discuss their complementary aspects.

Ganellen, R. J. (1998). *Integrating the Rorschach and the MMPI-2 in Personality Assessment.* Manahasset, N.J.: Earlbaum.

The author presents the view that both the Rorschach and the MMPI-2 provide valuable information about an individual's symptoms, behavior, emotions, interpersonal functioning, self-concept, defenses, and dynamics. He reviews the recent debate on whether the data from the two instruments is, or should be, convergent. Chapters presenting clinical material are especially helpful to the new Rorschacher.

Handler, L., & Hilsenroth, M. J. (Eds.) (1998). *Teaching and learning personality assessment.* Mahwah, NJ: Lawrence Erlbaum Associates.

This is a very comprehensive textbook on personality assessment with only a partial focus on the Rorschach, but the section "Teaching and Learning Specific Test Instruments," particularly the chapters by Irving Weiner and Virginia Brabender, are very helpful guidelines to students of the Rorschach as well as instructors.

Krawer, J. S., Lerner, H.D., Lerner, P. M., and Sugarman, A. (1980). *Borderline Phenomena and the Rorschach.* New York: International Universities Press, Inc.

This edited book describes Borderline Personality Organization in adults and children, and illustrates the assessment of BPO with the Rorshach. It is particularly helpful to the advanced student who has mastered basic personality assessment and Rorschach interpretation. It offers a structured way to assess defense mechanisms, and a cogent review of objects relations theories and Rorschach phenomena.

Leichtman, M. (1996). *The Rorschach: A developmental perspective.* Hillsdale, NJ: Analytic Press.

Leichtman discusses the Rorschach as a measure of representation in which perceptions and associations combine to produce a response. He writes from a psychoanalytic perspective, illustrating the developmental genesis of particular scores. This is helpful to both the assessment of children and adults, and supports an often-stated argument that in order to understand adult psychology and psychopathology you must understand the development of personality.

Lerner, H. D., & Lerner, P. M. (1988). *Primitive mental states and the Rorschach*. Madison: International Universities Press, Inc.

This is another advanced text for the Rorschach student who wants to understand more about object relations and defense mechanisms. There are several chapters on Narcissistic Personality Disorder, Cooper and Arnow's discussion of the psychology of the self, and an early work on the Rorschachs of women with histories of incest.

Lerner, P. M. (Ed.) (1996). Special Series: The nature of the Rorschach task and of interpretation. *J. Pero Assessment, 67*(3), 462–500.

Meloy, J. R. (1991). Rorschach testimony. *J. of Psychiatry & Law*, Fall–Winter, 221–235.

Meloy presents simple guidelines for expert witnesses who testify about the scientific data generated by the Rorschach. He advises the test user to avoid overinterpretation of the data, and makes suggestions for protecting the test materials in court.

Meyer, G. J. (Ed.) (1999). Special series on the utility of the Rorschach for clinical assessment. *Psychological Assessment, 11(3)*.

Five articles which debate the research about the utility of the Rorschach. Authored by what Meyer describes as "the primary advocates and critics" of the Rorschach. Included are articles by Stricker and Gold on the unique contribution of the Rorschach to assessment; Viglione on the strengths and limitations of the Rorschach in clinical assessment; Hunsley and Bailey on limitations in utility and validity of the Rorschach in clinical assessment; Hiller, Rosenthal, Bornstein, Berry and Brunell-Neulib, presenting a metanalysis of the Rorschach and the MMPI; and Dawes on principles that guide reseachers to examine incremental validity.

Weiner, I. B. (1996). Some observations on the validity of the Rorschach Inkblot Method. *Psychological Assessment, 8*(2), 206–213.

Addressing criticisms leveled at the Rorschach by Dawes (1994) and others, Weiner reviews basic principles of validation of psychological tests and validity studies that are pertinent to the Rorschach, and that suggest that the Rorschach is at least as valid, for the purposes tested, as the MMPI. He summarizes a few selected lines of research that have consistently demonstrated the capacity of the Rorschach to measure observable phenomena, including Rorschach research on state v. trait variables, measuring developmental change in children, monitoring change in therapy, and measuring the symptoms of Post-Traumatic Stress Disorder.

Weiner, I. B. (1997). Current Status of the Rorschach Inkblot Method. *Journal of Personality Assessment, 68*(1), 5–19.

Weiner reviews the scientific, clinical, and professional status of the Rorschach in this article. He reviews the data base (e.g., normative and reference data) and data on interscorer agreement, and validity. The section on clinical status reviews some of the uses to which the Rorschach has been put (e.g., personality description, personality dynamics, differential diagnosis, treatment planning, behavioral prediction) and discusses the support for each, or lack thereof.

Weiner, I. B. (1998). *Principles of Rorschach Interpretation*. Lawrence Erlbaum Associates.

An invaluable book on interpretation that integrates structural, thematic, behavioral, and sequence analysis. Clinician friendly, the book provides systematic guidelines for describing personality functioning. The book is divided into three sections. Part I focuses on the empirical foundations in the inkblot method, Part II focuses on the elements of interpretation and, Part III presents ten case illustrations.

Weiner, I. B., & Exner, J. E. (1991). Rorschach changes in long-term and short-term psychotherapy. *Journal of Personality Assessment, 56,* 453–465.

The authors outline Rorschach scores that measure stress tolerance, ideation, affect modulation, feelings about self and relationships with others, and present data from several hundred short-term therapy patients and over eighty long-term patients. The variables they suggest (summarized in Chapter 7, Clinical Applications) present a structured and data-based method for evaluating foci of therapy interventions and change in psychotherapy.

Weiner, I. B., Exner, J. E., & Sciara, A. (1996). Is the Rorschach welcome in the courtroom? *Journal of Personality Assessment, 67*(2), 422–424.

The authors survey 7,934 recent federal and state court cases in which psychologists presented Rorschach testimony. In only six of these was the appropriateness of the Rorschach challenged, and in only one of these cases was testimony not admitted. The authors conclude "there is accordingly good reason to believe that, despite occasionally voiced concerns to the contrary, the Rorschach is welcome in the courtroom."

Zillmer, E. A, Harrower, M., Ritzler, B., A., & Archer, R. P. (1995). *The quest for the Nazi personality: A psychological investigation of Nazi war criminals.* Lawrence Erlbaum Associates.

This book is an illustration of applied Rorschach research. It is an example of the richness of the Rorschach and provides a historical perspective of the test and basic constructs from social, development, and clinical psychology. Included are Rorschach protocols taken from Nazi war criminals gathered for the Nuremberg Trials. Surrounding the theme of "the myth of the Nazi Personality," the authors present individual protocols and case studies (of Karl Donitz and Julius Streicher) as well as a sample of Danish collaborators' Rorschachs. They carefully illustrate their point that though there was no single personality type among Nazi war criminals. The Rorschach reveals the abnormalities of personality that made the participants' role in the Nazi organization possible. The politics of obtaining the Rorschach records and the Nuremberg trials and evaluations of Nazi defendants are, in themselves, a fascinating study.

Index